How To Sell Your House Quick In Any Market

A Complete Guide To Marketing, Repairs & Offering Seller Financing

By: Stuart Modeen

With: Dan Quade

Edited By: Steven Pohl

Contents

Part III Seller Financing- The Best Thing To Do In A Slow Market

Part IV Creative Ways to Get Rid of Your House & Avoid Foreclosure

Bonus Section

Introduction

We live in a very economically challenging time in history. The housing market has gone from boom to bust in many parts of the country. I am an optimist though, and that is what I hope you become after reading through my book. Everyone's situation is different and life at times looks very bleak, trust me I have been through the hard times also. Although I have been on the brink of having to file bankruptcy, I have avoided it by overcoming the obstacles facing me. Through it all I have stayed optimistic and along with my attitude and my deep faith in God I have gotten through those difficult times. I sincerely hope that the information I am providing helps you to sell your house quickly, no matter the reason you are wanting or needing to sell. I am an investor and want you to learn from my experiences. I have learned some very important lessons along the way. To the fellow investor who may be reading this as a helpful tool in selling houses that you are flipping, I wish you the best of luck and urge you to keep working towards your goals and dreams as the market will rebound. To those who feel stuck in their situation and are having a hard time finding motivation, I'm telling you to get off the couch. Find your motivation, whether it be to avoid foreclosure or simply because you want to sell or to move to another city. Once you know your motivation then take action. You can analyze your situation to death and still not be any closer to your goal a week, a month or a year from now if you don't take action. If you want to sell your house bad enough then take action. I can guide you and give you tips that will help.

Just like many other people I started out with almost nothing. I came from a lower middle class family in a blue collar town where the economy has been depressed for years. I am an average person just like you, with a job and a family trying to make it. I own rental property and I have also bought and sold properties. I have learned a good part of what I know from other people. Utilizing knowledge from others has been a big contributor to my success.

I apply what I learn and I have used the power of leverage in my investing. Most people have an inspiration, a defining moment or person who changed their life for the better. My inspiration was Carleton Sheets. I was renting an apartment being newly married and having just found a somewhat decent job. We stayed up late watching tv most nights because I worked 2nd shift. Since nothing else good was on tv I would watch over and over again the Carleton Sheets infomercial. I would tell my wife that these people are no smarter than me. Even though we had very little money some of the people sharing testimonies had started with less than we had. We decided to buy the course. However, I must admit that I am very frugal and you have to be when you don't have much money so instead of paying several hundred dollars ordering the course off the infomercial I bought a slightly older version on Ebay for a fraction of the price.

My wife and I decided to buy our first home several blocks from where we were renting. We didn't have enough money for the down payment and closing costs. We asked the seller to pay part of the closing costs and then we went to a local bank and borrowed money against our car that we owned free and clear to come up with the rest. On our income we couldn't make the payments on a single family house so we had decided to become landlords and buy a duplex. We rented out the upstairs and lived downstairs for a couple years. When our income had increased we decided to buy a single family home for ourselves. We found a HUD foreclosure just 2 blocks away that was an excellent deal and fit our affordability for monthly house payments. We had to put some work into it. However, my wife and I aren't afraid of learning. We went from being renters to landlords and having our own house. We went from not knowing how to deal with a clogged sink to learning how to lay down floor-ing, put up sheetrock, install light fixtures and many other things. Don't be afraid to learn. Learning from this book, the internet, and other books on selling houses and other people are going to contribute to your success at selling your house. Don't feel that you need to do this alone. I couldn't possibly have accomplished what I have if it weren't for the help and advice of friends, realtors, real-estate investment buddies and my mortgage broker. Some of these selling techniques I have used and others I have learned about from people who have done them. Read my book. Figure out which plan of action is best for your situation. If you get it wrong the first time then try something else. I listed a house with a realtor who couldn't get it sold but then I changed to another realtor who sold it very quickly. I have also listed a house with 2 realtors who couldn't sell it but then I sold it very quickly on a contract for deed. Just as I have done I urge you to plug ahead, stay optimistic. Remember, work hard, be creative and get help from others as much as possible. Apply the techniques in this course to get your house sold quickly!

Getting help from others is vital to having success. Many ideas and selling techniques in this book came from my good friend Dan Quade. He owns First Star Property Group which is a real-estate investment company and he has flipped many properties. He is a seasoned real-estate investor who has bought and sold many properties creatively. On most of the houses he sold he offered seller financing and put together his own advertising. You will see examples of his creative advertising techniques in this book. Dan likes to think outside the box when it comes to buying and selling houses. He believes in always having a back-up plan and to advertise, advertise, advertise. Dan's ads are so unique that they stand out from the pack and get his phone ringing off the hook each and every time. Learn from his success and find people around you who can contribute to your success in reaching your goal of selling your house.

Preparing Your House For Sale

The 90 Day Rule

Developing your strategy is very important when selling your house. You need to decide if you are going to sell it yourself or hire a realtor. Either way you go I would recommend that you follow any of the techniques listed in this book for no longer than 90 days. If you haven't sold your house in that amount of time then you really need to do 3 things. First, is you need to look at your asking price and consider a price drop especially if you haven't done one yet. I personally recommend at least a 5% or more drop in price for it to be noticed. Lowering your price by $2000 which is 1% on a $200,000 house isn't going to be noticed by anyone. Many times a house will get an offer within 4 weeks of being new on the market as long as the price is right and the house is cosmetically appealing, and most realtors will recommend doing a price drop after just 30 days. I agree with this and highly highly recommend a price drop after 30 days as sometimes that is all that's needed for someone who walked through your house to put that offer in. At the very least, if your house is priced right and there is nothing wrong with it, then you should have gotten a good number of showings and a couple second showings. Second showings are very impor-tant as these are people that liked the house enough to at least give it a second look. This means your house is on their narrower list of places they are considering buying.

Second, you should rethink who is selling your house and how it's marketed. If you have it listed with a realtor then maybe you want to list it with a different agent and with a different agency. Maybe you want to dump the realtor and try selling the house yourself. If you have been trying to sell your-self and haven't had much luck then maybe you need to consider listing with a realtor or revamping your marketing plan. Marketing is everything when it comes to selling something whether it be a house, car, timeshare, boat, etc.

Third, you need to re-evaluate your home altogether. How do you stack up against comparables? Do all the comparables have a garage and you don't? Is your land-scaping in need of some revamping? Remember curb appeal is very important. What changes can you make to the inside or outside to add appeal? You don't get a second chance to make a first impression whether it be to people driving by the house or to those who you show the inside to. Your house must look its best if you are serious about selling it. If your house looks immaculate both inside and out then maybe you live in a declining neighborhood that most people don't want to buy in. The other possibility is that you live in a depressed real-estate market and you have done everything right, however the market situation which is beyond your control is preventing your house from selling. I believe you should still persevere and keep trying. Never give up! After each 90 day period try some-thing different, but the biggest and best change you can make is to offer seller financing. Banks are very tight on lending right now and if you offer seller financing you will find a buyer. The longer a house is up for sale whether it's through a realtor or a for sale by owner then the more stigma gets attached to the house and you will likely end up with a lower selling price. Some people keep a house listed with the same realtor for a year or longer but the more time that goes by the worse off you will be in the end.

Preparing Your House To Sell

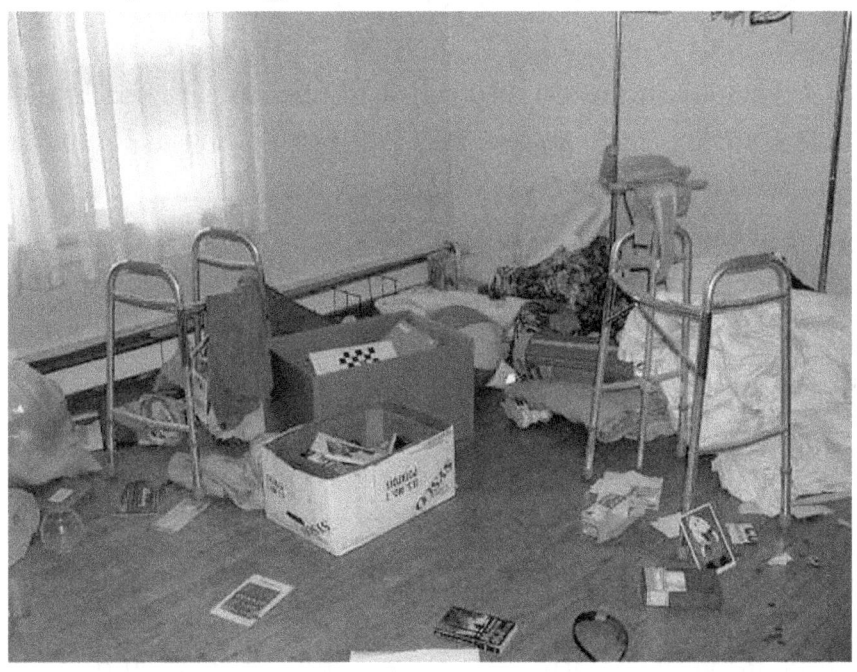

Get rid of your junk and clutter! This is going to be one of the most important things you do when selling your house. Nobody wants to walk through your basement or garage and see it stacked to the brim with clutter that you've accumulated over the last 10 years. Go through your things and bring anything that you are no longer using and that doesn't have sentimental value to the Goodwill or the Salvation Army. If you haven't used the item in over a year then get rid of it as the chances are that you won't use it ever again. Another option is to have a garage sale. If you decide that you just can't part with all these things and you really want to haul all that junk to your new house then rent a storage unit to keep it in for the meantime. Have a large attic? This is a good time to put it to use. After showing a house over and over again I noticed that no one asked to see the attic. Potential buyers asked how much insulation was up there but generally the only one who will see the attic is the home inspector that the buyer hires. I have found that stuffing your things in the attic is an exception to the rule of de-cluttering.

Organize your closets and make sure that your house looks as spacious as possible. If it looks crammed then potential buyers will perceive that the living space is too small for them. Yes, believe it or not but de-cluttered closets are very important as buyers look at them and make judgments. What I mean is that if a woman can't see that all her clothes would fit then this could be a real turn off. Are you not good at de-cluttering because you are so used to living with stuff everywhere or maybe you just don't know where to start or how to go about organizing? Then get a second opinion by a friend, relative or realtor on how to reorganize the rooms in your house to look more spacious and appealing. Remove the clutter off your walls. They don't need to be bare but be reasonable as some people have their walls covered everywhere with pictures, decorations, knick-knack shelves, etc. Keep a few pictures up, I recommend a mix of art work and some personal pictures to make it seem more like home. This goes for tables, end tables, coffee tables, dressers and any other furniture you have, remove knickknacks and have maybe only one item as a centerpiece if anything on each piece of furniture. Move your furniture around as necessary to make each room appear that it is spacious and if needed remove some furniture if the room still looks too crowded.

The exterior of your house needs to have the same de-cluttering done. On the outside of your house you must have curb appeal. This simply means that the house makes a good first impression when potential buyers take a drive by. Don't have your kid's toys laying all over the yard. The outside needs to look just as organized and neat as inside and maybe even more so. Landscape, plant flowers, keep the grass mowed, put a fresh coat of paint on the garage or shed, etc. Keep the family dog somewhere that it's not visible to potential buyers driving by. Nothing makes a worse first impression than Fido in the front yard barking at everyone and pooping on the sidewalk. When you have a showing please take your dog out of the house with you. You don't want to turn someone off from your house due to a dog constantly barking in a bedroom closet. They will go home and when they are pondering their decision about which house to buy the only thing they will remember about your house is the annoying dog. Trust me as I have looked at many houses with annoying pets. I have also looked at houses with dog poop all over the yard and needless to say that I have never bought, nor did I remotely consider buying one of these houses so I urge you to please clean this up. Make sure to trim hedges, cut down dead or overgrown trees and make sure the yard overall looks appealing. Fences must be kept up as well so if you have one and its wood then paint or stain it and if it's metal make sure it's presentable. Pull all weeds and anything else necessary out of your metal fence and put weed killer along the bottom of the whole fence if necessary. These small things really go a long way. Just remember you won't get a second chance to make that first impression.

Tip: The biggest way to add to curb appeal is to cut down trees and shrubs that are blocking the view of the front of your house.

Spend a little money and improve your house cosmetically. This small investment can pay off big time. The first thing I would recommend doing is to remove all wallpaper. Not only is wallpaper out of style but no two people have the same taste when it comes to wallpaper. Plus if it's a bedroom that you used as a nursery and you had kid's wallpaper up that could clash with the buyer who is going to use it for an office and would therefore rip it down anyway. Most people don't have vision. The average buyer comes in and sees a nursery that you created, not the office they would create. First time home buyers tend to be young people and they usually hate wallpaper. Many first time homebuyers are lazy and don't want to spend hours tearing your wallpaper off the walls. My parents have a nice house that they tried selling but the comments they would get is there is just too much wallpaper in the house.

Paint, carpet and tile your entire house with neutral colors. Get rid of orange and blue and pink and purple and paint everything beige or another neutral color. I would just avoid white as it's not very appealing in my mind. The only exceptions to this would be is if you have a small room and you need to make it look bigger or a basement then painting it white may help with adding a more spacious or clean look. After you paint the next thing you need to do is rip out old carpet. Buyers, especially if they are first time homebuyers, get excited over new carpet. It doesn't have to be top of the line just new, and again stick with a neutral color for the carpet as well. Right now the frieze carpet is the popular thing. I personally love and have used it and the house I live in also has it. If you have vinyl tile in your kitchen or bathroom that is from the 70's or has seen better days then replace this also. The kitchen and bathroom are the most important rooms so make them as appealing as possible. When trying to figure out where you will get the most bang for your buck when remodeling then look at the statistics on the following page.

According to Remodeling Magazine here are the top 10 improvements and your expected cost recovery at resale:

1. Minor Kitchen Remodel   91%
2. Bathroom Remodel   89%
3. Replace Siding   82%
4. Bathroom Addition   79%
5. Family Room Addition   78%
6. Replace Windows   67%
7. Master Suite   62%
8. Major Kitchen Remodel   58%
9. Sunroom Addition   58%
10. Deck Addition   54%

As you can see the kitchen and bathroom are the important rooms on the inside and the siding, windows and deck are what's important to buyers on the outside. Take some of my experiences into account when thinking of ideas to remodel your house. I have looked at many houses that still have carpet in the kitchen or bathroom which is a very outdated look. Laminate, which is the snap together flooring, is economical which is why it's catching on more and more and it's easy to install (trust me, if I can learn to do this then anyone can). In the previous house we lived in we decided to go carpet free and we put laminate flooring in our whole house except the bathrooms. We even put laminate up the stairway and it looked really nice. They even make laminate flooring for kitchens and bathrooms that look like squared tiling. Most hardware stores sell a "How To" video if you aren't comfortable attempting this without first gaining some knowledge. These videos are very helpful as they show you step by step how to do your project. Besides the fact that laminate floors look nice the other reason I like them is they get rid of carpet which holds dust mites and dirt and for some people causes allergies.

For other ideas you can go to your local hardware store and get brochures if you need ideas or your local bookstore and browse through magazines or books. Otherwise watch 'Flip This House' or 'Design To Sell' on HGTV or check out their website for ideas. The internet can be a great resource when it comes to ideas that won't cost a lot but make a real difference in adding cosmetic appeal. Just remember, that on the internet you will be able to find cutting edge ideas and see what other people out there are doing. Are you more hands on and want to go walk around the store to get ideas? If so, I personally recommend going to IKEA if you have one near you. Both my wife and I absolutely love that store. We both love the modern look and they have so many decorating ideas and choices of things that you can buy and put together yourself.

One of the most important areas for a kitchen is the cabinets. If they look old and worn but are still very solid then consider refinishing them. This can be a lot easier than you think. Generally painting them white or black depending what look you are going for and changing the hardware will improve their appeal immensely. Just make sure you don't buy just any paint, ask someone at your hardware store what kind of paint they recommend for this. I personally like using Behr paint from Home Depot, as it's one of the best quality paints out there but still affordable. You also might be able to re-stain the cabinets depending on their condition. Make sure to decide what look you are going for. My wife has refinished cabinets by painting them black and putting sleek silver hardware to create a modern look. She has also painted cabinets white and put silver hardware to create more of a country look. Depending how bad the cabinets are you might end up having to replace them. If you do then there are a lot of options available. Menards and IKEA both have good selections depending on your needs and the look you are going for. Be very careful not to over do it. What I mean is don't put super high end cabinets in a $100,000 first-time buyer type of house. Select cabinets that are appropriate to the overall style you are creating for the kitchen and appropriate for the price you will get for the house otherwise you may not recover very much of your investment.

Here is a couple pictures of a kitchen in a house we bought to remodel before we did any work to it.

Here is the same kitchen after remodeling. The total cost was less than $1000 but the cosmetic improvement was immense.

I highly recommend replacing the counter top unless you have a neutral one already that's still in excellent shape. If it's orange or looks like it's from the 80's or older then no matter how good of shape it's in you better toss it. One way around this is you can buy countertop overlays which go over the existing counter and give it a whole new look. As crazy as it sounds, I have heard stories of people not buying a house just because of the color of the countertop even if they liked everything else about the house. Many people buying a house today either don't know how to or don't want to have to change things, they just want to move in and have everything be perfect. Countertops can be bought very inexpensively at Menards so highly consider doing this.

In the bathroom make sure everything is spotless. Remove any old caulk and replace with new stuff. Be neat when caulking otherwise people will notice especially women (my wife notices my horrible caulking job every time). Depending how much you want to spend and how outdated your bathroom is it might be worthwhile to replace the bathtub and sink along with the vanity and maybe even the toilet. This is a very small detail but make sure the toilet is spotless for showings. Many people will look at this and yes they may even use your toilet if nature is calling so make sure that it's not disgusting. If you have an old claw foot tub then consider replacing it unless your house is an old Victorian style house. The claw foot tubs are coming back in style but make sure the feel of the whole bathroom goes along with it. I have learned that most people want to be able to take a shower so this works most ideal if you have 2 bathrooms. One bathroom could have a shower and the other a claw foot tub. The first house I ever sold house got a lot of showings but took quite awhile to sell because of this issue. There was only one bath-room with a claw foot tub and no room to change it to a shower because the ceiling was slanted. I did think about knocking out walls to expand

the bathroom but that would have been quite an investment. The bathroom in that house was also small so that
didn't help. Eventually the house sold as is to a neighbor
who was tired of renting.

Picture of bathroom with slanted ceiling.

Change out the light fixtures. This doesn't cost very
much but can really make a huge difference when trying to
give your house a more updated look. Replace the Victorian
chandelier in the dining room with something more modern.
Go to Menards or Home Depot and you will be amazed at the

affordable choices for new light fixtures. Generally in bedrooms I recommend to put in the glass dome lights which
usually sell for around $10 each and sometimes less. If you
have a higher end home and would like to spend a little more
then you can usually find decent fixtures for under $100. I
wouldn't spend anymore than that as you will never recover
that extra cost when selling.

   The walls in your house and the ceiling are also very
important. Buyers will run if they see cracks in either. It's
not very hard nor is it time consuming to patch walls so
make sure you fix any cracks you see and fill in any nail
holes. Joint compound and spackle are both very cheap so
there is no reason to not do this. Between the two I recommend joint compound as it's more durable. I have also
found that spackle tends to discolor when it's painted over
thus making it noticeable where you patched the wall. To
avoid this, make sure that you prime the areas you patched
before painting. Make sure to also fix spots where paint is
peeling. This is vitally important, not just for look, but also
depending on the age of the house there could be lead based
paint.

   The outside of the house will be the first impression so
make sure it is cosmetically appealing. Paint any trim that
needs touching up and don't forget about the deck as a re-
staining or a fresh coat of paint can make a real difference.

If there are cracks in the driveway then fix them also and maybe the garage may need a fresh coat of paint or a crack-ed window needs replacing. Fix broken steps and railings. Finally replace burnt out bulbs and make sure all outdoor lights are working. For some good ideas on sprucing up the outside of the house to make it look appealing you can watch HGTV.

If you decided you are willing to improve the house before you sell it then I would most heavily focus on the kitchen and bathroom. However, if you already have a nice interior then I would think about replacing some windows if they are old or putting on a deck if you don't have one. The great thing about doing windows is Uncle Sam is currently offering tax rebates on a portion of your investment to put more energy efficient windows in. Some areas that I don't recommend to invest money on if you don't have to (and you might have to if these things have big issues) are replacing the roof, a new furnace, installing new plumbing or wiring, or anything else that's has to do more with mechanics than cosmetics. Again if any of these things are in really bad shape then you may need to do something about them. The reason behind this is the payback on your investment is going to be very little. Sure the buyer will appreciate that you did these things but they aren't going to add much value to the house. One area that many people who are selling sometimes neglect but shouldn't is the basement. If your basement isn't finished off then I'm not saying that you need to do this unless all the others in the neighborhood that are for sale are. However, you should if possible make sure it's as bright and clean as possible. Don't over do it as it's just the basement but if its dark and dreary then I would recommend to paint the walls white and paint the floor a darker color like gray or brown. If your basement leaks then buy the waterproofing paint and slap a couple coats on to reduce the leakage. People really hate leaky basements. A good word of advice is when the neighbors are having an open house then go in and see their house. To give yourself the best chance of selling you should see how your house stacks up to the neighbors. Make adjustments as necessary but don't go overboard. If the other houses for sale in the neighborhood all have a deck then you should probably add one. However if the neighbors all have new plumbing and you don't then I wouldn't bother with this.

Staging

Stage your house. This is a fairly new concept and is catching on more in the big cities and the west coast. I highly recommend trying it and in a competitive housing market it could really improve your chances of selling quicker. If you don't have a good eye for decorating then find a friend or family member who does. On the internet there are many sites with great ideas or you could watch 'Design To Sell' for ideas. Spend a day at IKEA walking through their massive showroom for ideas on the latest trends. Don't have an IKEA near you? Go online to ikea.com. If you haven't heard of IKEA before, it's a huge store that sells household furniture and accessories. The cost of the items there are very reasonable as all the furniture such as end tables, coffee tables, etc. come in flat boxes and you bring them home and assemble it yourself. Most of what IKEA sells is modern looking and stylish and will fit most peoples budgets. A few other stores that tend to sell trendier things that could be used as props are Target, Pier One, and TJ Maxx. You could also hire a professional staging company but depending on your selling price or potential profit this might not be worth it. All staging is is decorating your house in a way that a buyer could see the house as where they want to live. Basically you are creating an atmosphere that says, 'buy me'. You are giving them a preview of the lifestyle they want to live and a house that they could see themselves as calling home. A lot of this can be small stuff like having fragrant candles burning for an open house. In the bathroom fold washcloths and a towel in a decorative fashion with a brand new bar of soap on top. Have a pot of flowers on the dining room table, either fake or real is fine. Put decent pictures up on the walls in each room and make sure to remove any family ones. People like to see pictures or artwork of nature not your family. Get a few plants either real or fake to put in a couple corners of the house. Have a barbecue grill sitting on the deck. Put a cookie jar or a glass pitcher with kitchen utensils sitting in it on the kitchen counter. Have tea light or other candles burning along with classical music playing for showings.

Use your imagination. The key here is that everything appears neat and not cluttered. Staging may be easier if you still live in the house because if you've moved out then you would need to bring some furniture back in so the house doesn't look bare. I don't recommend leaving your house empty unless you have to. If possible I would recommend putting at least a dining room table, couch, bed and dresser in the house. Again just make sure the house doesn't look completely empty and bare nor do you want your staging to look in such a way that someone will think that you forgot a few things when you moved out. When staging make sure to use as new of stuff as possible as shoddy furniture will just defeat the purpose and possibly leave a bad impression. You may want to go out and buy some new furniture that you will leave with the house as a way to entice buyers. A group of house flippers in my area buys a nice brand new couch that they leave for the buyers. Depending on your market, staging might not be necessary. For instance, if your house is in bad condition anyway then its not going to make a difference or if the selling price is really low then it might not make a difference either. However if you have a nice house and want to increase appeal, then staging is a great way to increase interest and push someone over the edge toward buying. Plus it may increase the perceived value of your house and might lead to multiple offers and a higher selling price or at the very least a quicker sale.

Have your target buyer in mind when selling. The general appeal that you create from doing cosmetic improvements and staging must work together to go hand in hand with what your buyer is looking for. For instance if your house is a lower priced house in your market and you think you may attract a young couple then maybe you want to do everything with a modern appeal. This might mean painting the kitchen cabinets black and putting sleek silver hardware on them as well as modern light fixtures throughout the house. If you have a higher priced house that might attract a professional like a doctor or lawyer then maybe you would want to install a granite countertop, a dishwasher and stainless steel appliances. For both examples make sure the decorations go along with these themes. Remember your style of decorating might not be theirs. For instance if you like Victorian style decorating then you should probably remove all your decorations unless you have a historic house then it might be appropriate. Make sure the house is so appealing that it creates an emotional reaction from buyers when they walk in. The house that I live in now had just that feel for my wife and I the first time we saw it. We had viewed many houses prior to this one. When we walked in we both looked at each other and said, "I want this house".

Another point to keep in mind when thinking of your potential buyer is that the woman is usually the one with the final say. Therefore the house needs to be appealing to a woman. My wife would never let me buy a house if she didn't like it and rightfully so as she spends more time at home than I do. It's important to a woman for the house to feel like home. Though the largest group of first time homebuyers tends to be couples there are now 22% of first time homebuyers that are single women. Only 9% are single men. So if you take 22% of the market + factor in that women are the key decision maker for most couples out there then you have a really large share of the market. I don't know how much clearer I can make my point but you must make sure your house appeals to women. There are some extra special ways you can do this such as getting fresh flowers and putting them in a vase on the table or counter, burn nicely scented candles and do anything else possible to make sure there is a pleasant aroma in the house. If the house stinks like rotting garbage, cigarette smoke or sometimes even a pet then buyers will run as fast as they can in the opposite direction. One of the first investment properties I ever bought stunk immensely. Why did I buy it? Everyone else ran therefore making the price rock bottom. I knew that it was simply spoiled food in the fridge that was causing this horrible odor and the sellers didn't really care because it was kind of an estate sale situation. After I bought the house I cleaned the fridge out really well and then put baking soda in it to neutralize the smell. I opened the windows to air out the house and painted the walls and got the house smelling good again. I also bought another house that not only stunk like cigarette smoke but the walls were all yellowed. Needless to say I got a good deal as no one else wanted the house. Moral of the story, make sure the house smells good. Again keep your target buyer and their tastes in mind not yours and try to make the house appeal to as many people as possible.

Staging From A Woman's Perspective

Since the woman is usually the one with the final decision on the house I thought it best to have a woman's perspective on staging and creating an inviting atmosphere. Here are some of my wife's thoughts on the topic. Just as they say on 'Designed To Sell' "just good enough isn't good enough" and you need to put forth an effort when staging and creating appeal for your buyer. Study your competition and go to open houses to see what other sellers are doing and then make changes to ensure your house stands out from the crowd. On the outside add flowers to the porch to create more curb appeal and make the house more inviting. The front door has to look good. Depending on the selling price and condition of the door it may need to be replaced and at the very least make sure the doorknob looks good. Inside the house envision the kind of buyer your house is suited for and think how to appeal to that group of buyers. Make sure that every room has a purpose. If you have a third bedroom being used as a computer room then remove the computer and add a bed and dresser to show that it's a third bedroom. Remove the litter box and ash trays. Clean, clean and clean some more. If you are still living in the house you may need to change some of your daily habits to fit this as your house needs to remain ready to be shown at a moments notice. To do this you need to make the beds every morning, wash the dishes right away after every meal, wash the dirty laundry everyday, keep the house picked up, clean sinks, toilets and the bathtub frequently. The most important of these is to keep the kitchen sink clean as a dirty sink is a huge turn off. Do you have a garbage disposal and want to ensure it smells ok? Simply put half a lemon down there and you will give your kitchen a fresh lemon aroma. Keep the toothbrushes and other personal hygiene items put away. Go through every room and remove unnecessary things and put them in storage. This could mean eliminating 70% of what's in your house. The house needs to appear that there is lots of storage and space especially to walk. The smaller the house the smaller the furniture will need to be and closer together to give the appearance of spaciousness. The house needs to have a good flow so the less furniture the better. Only keep out those few select items that look good. For the dining room a chandelier and the table is all that needs to be in that room. In the bedroom closet only keep a few clothing items that match by color and do not pack the closet full of stuff as potential buyers will notice. A tip I advise you follow when selling your house is to stay away from the shopping malls as the goal is to de-clutter not to keep buying. For the living room add some accent color items like pillows to the couch and artwork on the wall (you can find all that inexpensive at your local home decorating store) that coordinate well with the wall color. Paint the house in neutrals but make sure the colors aren't too boring. In the living room if you have a fireplace or a bay window then you need to showcase that and make it the focal point by removing everything away from it and making it the center. Nice hardwood floors should also be showcased. The more you can draw attention to the positives about the house and distract from the negatives the better. Final thoughts would be to have the house smelling good and fresh. Just before showings I recommend to open the windows even if the weather means you can't leave them open, at least get some fresh air in the house. Then burn candles and make cookies for your potential buyers, which also gets the house smelling good and don't forget to remove personal items like grandma's urn before the showing.

Here is a picture of a staged living room. Notice how everything in the room has a purpose. The curtains, pillows, end table, coffee table, lamp, rug and dressers all came from IKEA. The couch, loveseat and chair came from a furniture store. I would recommend adding some art work on the walls so they don't look bare.

Create More Living Space to Add Value

Many sellers today are in a situation where they have little or no equity in their house, but even if you do I still recommend to examine your house and create additional living space if possible. This adds to the value and the overall appeal of the house. The best opportunity for this is usually finishing off your basement if you have one. If you decide that you must finish the basement, then I highly recommend to add at least a quarter bath containing a toilet and a sink as people tend to go nuts over this. Make sure that you show what this new space is to be used for. If you create a big open space then if possible put a pool table or something to show the buyers that this can be an excellent game room. Dividing part of the space is usually helpful. If there is no garage or very little storage then maybe you will want to create a storage room along with a game room. You could maybe even create a nice little office. Also remember the more bedrooms a house has the better. If you have a 2 bedroom house and you are able to change the layout to a 3 bedroom then that is going to make a big difference value wise. Have a huge basement? Add an extra bedroom or two. Don't have a basement? Look to see how big your existing bedrooms in the house are as it might make sense to divide one of them into 2 bedrooms. This isn't always the case but things you might want to consider. Do you have a large extra space above your garage that could be finished off? Now is the time to do just that. A realtor should be able to give you good feedback on some of this as to what they have seen that helps and what doesn't in your area.

Repair It Yourself Or Hire Professional Help

At some point before listing your house or after you have found a buyer but prior to close there is a good chance you will end up doing some repairs. If you aren't very knowledgeable in building material costs then it would be a good idea to bring a friend or relative or maybe a contractor you trust to look at it and estimate how much in material would be needed if you did everything yourself. This is not a time to experiment with learning how to do something yourself, especially if it's a repair the home inspector pointed out. Trying to save some money could end up costing you a lot more if you are incompetent to do the work correctly. The last thing you want is to think you fixed the problem only to get that dreaded phone call 3 months later that the house is having that same issue again because you did a shoddy job. If it's a simple fix or something that you know you can for sure handle without a doubt in your mind and correct your-self then go ahead and do it and maybe have someone assist you if needed. Only you know your limits. I always want to make sure repairs and renovations are done correctly there-fore I do what I know how to do like paint & patch walls, replace flooring, replace toilets and bathroom vanities. There are some things that I feel uncomfortable doing like roofing (it doesn't help that I am afraid of heights), wiring, plumbing, and window replacement. I have hired contractors in the past both to do work and sometimes to assist me.

Once you have determined that you need to hire a contractor then make sure to get at least 3 bids for your project. To ensure that you get the job done to your expectations then always get the bid in writing. I recom-mend never accepting a verbal offer as its usually only fly by night contractors that do these. When something is in writing you know exactly what the contractor is going to cover as far as labor and materials. Professional contractors give an accurate estimate and never charge more. Referrals are great and in my mind necessary as not all contractors are reputable or fast at finishing the job. Just because someone offers you the lowest price their quality and speed of work might not be the greatest. There is a great website called angieslist.com that allows you to check up on contractors from chimney sweepers to driveway repair contractors to handymen to plumbers and everything in between. In most areas of the country this website charges a fee however it's an excellent resource so I recommend using it. The reason is they compile reports from consumers both good and bad who have used contractors in your area so this will give you insight in who to avoid and who will give you piece of mind if you hire them. You can also check with your local Better Business Bureau or online at bbb.org. Due to the economy there are professional trades people like electricians, roofers, etc. who are out of work. Talk to family and friends and they may know of one of these professionals who is sitting in the unemployment line. If so then you may be able to save a bundle hiring them especially if it's during a slow time of the year like winter. Their price probably isn't set in stone either during these slow times so negotiate if you think the price they are charging is a little too high but don't be stingy as they need to make a living also. I know that its common sense but I am going to say it anyway, never pay a contractor until the job is finished, period. If you do then likely you will find yourself having to pay a second person to come and finish the job. We have all done stupid things and even I made the mistake of paying a guy once before the job was completed. Well to make a long story short I made several phone calls and he made several promises to come but of course in the end he never came back. Make sure the contractor or person you hire is insured and bonded and also that they guarantee their work. You may even want to ask for names and phone numbers of people they have done work for so you can verify how good their work really is. Again you want peace of mind when you turn the keys over to your buyer. Let the contractor know the timeline you have to work with and tell them you can only hire them if they can guarantee being done by your specified date whether this is your closing date or the date that you need to get your house on the market. Don't procrastinate either. This is one of my biggest downfalls. I ended up in a situation in which I had to get a few small repairs done on my house before closing however I procrastinated. Thankfully I work with a very good contractor who also happened to be my neighbor a few years ago. He came to my rescue and finished the repairs in the morning on the day I was supposed to close and while the buyers were doing their final walk through. Talk about a close call.

Selling Your House With A Realtor

So you decided you are going to sell your house and you want to go the traditional route and hire a realtor. Time is of the essence and you want to find a good realtor and do it fast. Choosing the right person for this job can be challenging; just like in every profession there are the ones that do a good job and well, not so impressive ones. I have learned the hard way and worked with both. So how do you pick and choose who will best fit your needs among hundreds of people which one is right for you? First, you may know a realtor personally or through a friend, family member or co-worker. Going the referral route like this or picking someone you already know needs to be done with extra care as you may already have a favorable view of the agent without knowing how good of a salesperson they are. Referrals from someone might be good or they might not. Remember we are looking for fast results here. Here is how I recommend to pick the best realtor for selling your house:

The most important thing for getting your house sold quickly is advertising. I recommend to look at who is advertising their listings the most in your local newspaper, on tv, on the web, in local house for sale magazines. You could choose a realtor that you found through a catchy ad they were running or by going to some open houses. The second thing you must do is test their level of communication by doing what I call the one phone call test. When you call a realtor see if they pick up the phone or if you get voicemail. If you get voicemail then leave a message. See how long it takes for them to get back to you. If they don't get back to you within 24 hours then don't bother with them. If you need to place more than one phone call to reach them then so would potential buyers therefore I recommend to run like the wind from these realtors. There is no excuse as communication is very important in sales. Good realtors even if they are out of town have an assistant taking their phone calls. If they are in classes or doing something else then they will be checking their messages and returning phone calls promptly. Other good realtors have a Blackberry to make sure both calls and emails are returned quickly. I highly recommend to test this theory on weekends. You wouldn't believe how many realtors out there don't work weekends especially at small discount agencies, as the saying goes you get what you pay for. I can't really blame them because neither do I. However, most people want to go look at houses on weekends not during the workweek. You could lose out on a lot of potential showings especially from out of town buyers if your realtor doesn't pick up their phone on weekends.

Now that the housing market is in the toilet a lot of realtors have also taken on second jobs and are selling houses only part time. Try to stay away from these part-timers as they aren't able to give full devotion and attention to getting your house sold since they have another job commitment. Once you have identified several good candidates who you think might be perfect for selling your house then bring each of them into your house. Invite them to come one at a time to give you a market analysis which is also referred to as a CMA or comparative market analysis. This is usually a free service that realtors offer that compares your house to others that have sold in your area recently that are similar to yours as well as existing homes on the market now. This will help determine a fair asking price for your house. If you are anything like me then you are probably saying to yourself right now that you don't need a realtor to pick a price for your house when you are perfectly capable of doing this yourself. This can be a big mistake as overpricing can mean your house sitting for months and under pricing means you might lose out on money you could have made. Be sure that your agent has either sold houses in your neighborhood before or has a good understanding of your neighborhood and the current real-estate market in your city. This can be crucial in getting your house sold faster as they will tell you exactly what you need to do for getting the right buyer. Some neighborhoods are more likely to attract only first time homebuyers and others are better neighborhoods that people are moving to after selling their previous house. Generally there are specifics about the price and aspects of the house that could be important for either scenario.

When the agents come over to your house you will need to interview them. First, ask them why they think you should hire them to sell your house. Next, ask them what their marketing plan is for selling your house. Also make sure you ask about their past results. Are they ranked as one of the top realtors in the area in terms of sales? Have they won any sales awards? How many houses have they sold in the last 6 months or 1 year? What is the average length of time their listings are on the market? How long have they been a realtor? Can they give you names and numbers of a few satisfied customers that you can call? How long of a contract do they require you sign with them? The longer the contract the more likely they don't get quick results. I recommend working with a realtor who will put you under contract for 3-4 months. If it's any longer than this then you could be over committing yourself to a mediocre realtor. Not to mention if it's a 3 month contract and you had a lot of showings and approved of the way the realtor was handling trying to sell your house then you have the flexibility of extending them another 3 months. If they didn't get people in the door then you have the option of going with someone else. I had a realtor list my house and try to sell it for 4 months but I got only a hand full of showings and they never brought their own clients into my house. Then when the contract ran out I found a different realtor to list with. When I listed with him I dropped the price $5000 and I got an offer in a week and a half. In that short amount of time he even got one of his own clients in my house. Make sure to ask about their guarantee because if the realtor isn't getting traffic through your house then you should have the option of canceling the contract early.

Realtors who advertise the most get the best results. Every agent will put your house in the MLS which is the Multiple Listing Service where it can be viewed by all the realtors in your area, so if this is all they mention for a marketing plan then you won't want to hire them. The world of advertising is always changing and almost all realtors list in the MLS, put a sign in the front yard and advertise in the local paper. This isn't enough. Instead find someone who will put your house on their company's website or the website of the local newspaper and also on realtor.com. It's free to list on craigslist.org so I recommend that your realtor does this, it may not lead to a sale but it might and since it's free there's nothing to lose. The web is becoming very big when first time homebuyers are searching for a home to buy. Ask the realtor to create what is called a virtual tour of your house by shooting a 360 degree video of your house that can be viewed on their website. This is becoming a popular thing and can be really helpful for out of town buyers who may be interested in buying your house. If your house is very appealing on the inside then this could be a real advantage to get more people wanting to look at your house. In some cases though it's usually the exception to the rule this virtual tour may sell your house with the buyer never coming for an actual showing. Most cities also have local real-estate for sale magazines that are free to the public and cheap to advertise in so make sure your realtor is advertising your house in there. Some realtors participate in weekly half hour programs where listings are showcased on tv generally on a Saturday or Sunday, so find out if your realtors company does this. Make sure your realtor advertises your house not just to the public but also to other realtors. The odds are that another realtor will end up selling your house to one of their buyers rather than your realtor. I recommend that you ask your realtor to have an open house that is only for other realtors (typically they will bring in all the agents that work in their office which is fine). I also recommend that you ask your realtor to send post cards with pictures of your house to other realtors. There are some really good agents that will also send post cards or fliers to other people they know including past clients to advertise their listings.

Watch out for realtors who are willing to give away your house to get it sold. Be sure to find out before signing that listing agreement that you have found out what their list to final selling price ratio is. This is simply the final selling price versus what it was originally listed at. An example would be that you have listed your house for $200,000 and the final selling price is $190,000 so $190,000/$200,000 is 95%. The higher the percent the better. It's very normal that it won't be 100%, as rarely does it happen that buyers pay 100% of the asking price unless it's a hot market. Everyone wants to get a good bargain so the price is usually negotiated down at least a little. If the agent is a good representative of their sellers though then this ratio will be very high. The best agents are good negotiators and will look out for your best interest and try to get you top dollar. Make sure you are also comfortable with the starting price as there are agents willing to start it a little low to get a sale. Going to a few open houses or just looking at a few listings in your neighborhood will help you determine that your realtor isn't listing your house too low to start. Again, picking a good realtor may be a bit of a challenge, but if you want quick results while also getting top dollar for your house then it's vitally important to hire only the best.

Once you have your realtor picked out then you need to structure the commission for maximum results. Most realtors will charge 4-6% to sell your house. Half of the commission usually goes to them and the other half to the realtor who represents the buyer. A lot of times the selling realtor will get more money and break down a 6% commission by taking 3.5% for themselves and giving 2.5% for the buyer's realtor. They justify this by saying that they are spending money on advertising. All of this is fine and good but again we are looking for maximum results. The odds are that a buyer's realtor is going to end up selling the house to one of their buyers not the selling realtor. When it does happen that the selling agent sells the house this is called dual agency but generally most houses are sold by another agent representing the buyer. I have never had a bad experience with a dual agency transaction but it does happen. The reason is that in these transactions the same realtor is representing both the buyer and the seller. To get more showings I recommend offering an extra incentive to a buyer's agent. You can do this anyway you want. A couple examples would be increasing the commission to 7% and splitting it equally between your realtor and the buyer's realtor. Another example would be a bonus of $1000 or $2000 to a buyer's agent if they sell your house. Think about it, realtors work on commission and if you were a realtor and knew that a certain house would give you an extra one or two thousand dollars on your paycheck, what house do you think you would want to show over and over again to your buyers? My best word of advice is not to be cheap on the commission. If you are selling a high end home then you may want to offer a free trip to a realtor that brings you a buyer. I know if I were a realtor and knew that I would get a free trip to Hawaii or Orlando if I made the sale then you better believe I would be bringing every prospective buyer I could to see that house (especially since I live in Minnesota where winter lasts forever!) The low priced real-estate agencies that will charge you 4% are generally discount brokerages. Unless you live in a hot market I wouldn't recommend listing with them as they generally advertise very little so you get what you pay for.

Help your realtor sell your house. I know this goes against the norm and also your desire not to be involved in the process of selling your house which is why you hired a realtor in the first place. Don't forget you are still getting support from a real-estate professional who is marketing your house, knows real-estate laws inside and out which will help keep you out of court, and they know market trends. Most states require realtors to have a certain amount of continuing education credits each year to keep their license. This is good as laws and trends change. However, desperate times call for desperate measures. What I mean by helping your realtor is there are several things you can do to assist your realtor in getting your house sold more quickly. Here are a few ways you can help:

1. The first and probably the most important is to be present when the house is shown. I don't mean sitting on the couch eating pizza and watching television. Doing something like this makes buyers feel very uncomfortable.

I have looked at houses where the seller was home but not engaged in showing me the property. Needless to say I never bought one of these properties. You don't need to be a salesman, all you have to do is to show the house to the prospective buyer. This is your opportunity to point out all the great things that you love about the house and all the improvements that you have made. Third parties such as a real estate agent don't have a personal interest in selling this particular property, so they will let the buyer in and most of the time the buyer shows themselves around. Just imagine how much more bragging you can do yourself by showing a potential buyer how your home can be a place that they could call home. Seeing the owner's pride of their house and the things they have done is more convincing. This will also give the buyer a chance to ask why you are selling. This is something people are curious about but generally don't get to ask when dealing only with realtors. I once bought a rental property that was for sale by owner because I had the opportunity to ask the seller directly the questions I had. Other properties that I looked at in which the owner showed me the house I considered buying whereas I might have otherwise ruled it out if only the realtor showed it. When I met the owner he seemed sincere, took great pride in all the improvements he made and he said the reason he was selling was due to retirement. Since this was a rental property this was very important for me to know as I felt a lot better that things have run smoothly for him with this property and also finding out that he owned the property for 13 years gave me piece of mind. He called it a turn key opportunity as there were new renters in both units with one year lease agreements so I was sold and ended up buying his property.

Another experience I had was when my wife and I were looking for our very first house. Our realtor invited the owner to be there and show us the house. We were able to get a complete picture of improvements that were made and some things that still needed to be done. Although we ended up not buying this house and choosing another it was solely because of the location. With that being said, it was one of the final houses we were considering, but if the owner hadn't shown it to us then we might have ruled it out right away. The only downside to being involved in showing your house is if the house has a lot of things wrong with it then you might feel embarrassed to show it. Be present for most showings can also be time consuming, especially if you get a lot of showings. When showing your house always focus only on the positives about the house but if someone asks you about a defect then be honest. Lying is wrong and could result in a lawsuit if something wasn't included on the disclosure. Being honest gives you more credibility and might increase your chance of a sale even if the buyer asks to knock something off the asking price to compensate for having to repair something. The other thing you can do is offer to have the repair taken care of before closing if they agree to purchase the house. The real estate market is very challenging right now and buyers are looking for houses that are near perfect. With this said please repair as many prob-lems before you list your house for sale.

2. The second thing you can do to assist your realtor is the obvious: keep the house clean and organized for showings. Be sure to keep the lawn mowed and the sidewalk shoveled which adds to the curb appeal. If your realtor points out something that might be a pitfall to a potential buyer then take their advice and fix it as soon as possible. Remember your realtor is a professional and they know best when it comes to knowing what might turn off a potential buyer. When dealing with a professional you need to listen to their advice as they know best from experience.

3. Another way you can assist the realtor is to throw in a bonus for a potential buyer. With the housing market crumbling to pieces there are many motivated sellers who have resorted to this. First, make sure your realtor has checked with your state's laws to find out what is legal or not for you to offer. Generally things inside the house are allow-ed. Most buyers will want to have your appliances so this is just a given. If your appliances are older and shoddy looking then I would seriously consider buying new ones. If you do go out and purchase brand new appliances then buy based on the selling price of the house. If you are trying to sell a

house in a lower income neighborhood to first time home-buyers then you wouldn't want to put stainless steel appliances in. Likewise, don't put bottom of the line in a house where you are trying to sell in a moderate to higher income neighborhood as you could end up turning off buyers just for this reason. I know it's kind of crazy but appliances really do matter to a lot of people. In addition to this, maybe you want to throw in a big screen tv, a barbecue grill, lawnmower, snow blower, carpet allowance, decorating allowance, new washer & dryer, etc. I have heard of sellers offering cars or exotic vacations but I would be wary of doing this as most lenders would be against it. Others are offering cash back at closing which can be illegal depending how it is done. The reason for the law is that the lender isn't putting out extra money to finance the buyer just so they can get a check back at closing. This increases their risk and may over-inflate the price of the house. There are times however that the buyer might legitimately end up with cash at closing such as security deposits being turned over to them on the purchase of an apartment building.

4. One thing you can do that virtually all sellers are doing is offer to pay part of the buyer's closing costs. The maximum that is usually allowed is 3% of the selling price but may vary by lender or program as to what is allowed. Make sure to figure this in when calculating how much you need to get out of the house. Take the following example,

let's say you are paying 3% of your buyers closing costs on a $100,000 house which equals $3000 plus you are paying a 6% commission to your realtor then that is another $6000 so add them together and you have $9000 being taken right off the top. Some sellers will increase their asking price once an offer is made to compensate for paying closing costs and this is usually allowed by lenders as long as the appraisal comes back fine so maybe you would agree to sell the buyer the house for $103,000 with you paying 3% of closing costs. In a hot market increasing the price for this might be an option but could be a lot harder in a tough market. It is important to think about your asking price and what you need to get out of the house when coming up with a listing price, as it may make more sense to try listing your house at $104,900. Just be aware that there are price ranges for buyers. Your realtor can tell you more about the ones in your local area. Here is a general example for a lower-priced housing market: the lowest group would be buyers who are looking for a house under $80,000. The next group up are buyers looking in the $80,000-$100,000 range. The next group up from them are looking for houses from $100,000-$120,000 and so on. If you list your house at $104,900 instead of $99,900 then you may have slowed down your chance at selling quick as you have decreased the number of buyers who would look at your house. Part of the reason for this is that when a buyer tells their realtor they only want to look at houses under $100,000 then that realtor is going to only e-mail them listings within that range. Likely the buyer is only able to borrow $100,000 from the bank so they would only ask for listings beyond this if they didn't find something they liked. Good realtors however will still inform their buyers of listings that are slightly over their maximum price as they can always try to negotiate down.

5. Finally, you may want to ask your realtor for permission to market your house yourself in addition to the marketing they are doing. This could potentially speed up your sale by increasing your home's exposure and, depending how you are advertising it, may not cost you very much. Realtors do advertise but they won't put your listing in the newspaper every week because they have other listings. They also can't have an open house for you every weekend either as they have other houses they are trying to sell. As long as you are still paying your agent the same commission whether you find the buyer or they do then they probably won't have an issue with it. You could try striking a deal if your advertising sells the house then you will deduct the cost of your ad off their commission.

Help-U-Sell Agencies

A Help-U-Sell agency is a realty company in which your house gets listed on the MLS and you pay a flat fee instead of a commission when the house sells. This is kind of an in between having a realtor and selling your house by yourself. These agencies assist you in helping you sell your house and they cost less than having your house listed with a realtor, but still giving you a lot of the same exposure. Typically these agencies do higher volumes of transactions then some agencies so they are very knowledgeable in handling the paperwork. Usually these agencies will have realtors working for them and since its on the MLS your house can be shown by a realtor who would get part of the fee that you paid. These agencies typically charge several thousand dollars so if you are selling a $200,000-$300,000 dollar house then this could be a real money saver versus paying a 6% commission to a realtor. The Help-U-Sell fee varies from agency to agency across the country as each are independently owned. They do brag that the average seller saves around $8000 so you get to keep more of your equity. Let's look at the example of Bob & Eleanor who are selling their house for $300,000 and a realtor quoted them a 6% commission which would be $18,000. They decide to list with Help-U-Sell which in their particular area charges a flat fee of $4000 so in the end they saved $18,000-$4000=$14,000. If you decide to go this route then make sure to discuss all fees that are involved because generally the agency will require you to purchase a certain amount of advertising also. This advertising usually consists of some of the same methods a realtor would use like advertising in the Sunday paper and the local real-estate magazine. Your house will appear in ads bearing the Help-U-Sell name along with other houses for people doing the same thing. They will even put a professional looking sign in your front yard. When I said "partnering" I meant is they are helping you sell the house but you are still doing some of the work yourself. You are holding your own open houses and aside from realtor show- ings you are showing the house to prospective buyers also. I have known people who have sold this way and were satis- fied with the results and the money they saved versus listing with a realtor. If you are the kind of person who wants to save some money but doesn't want to sell totally by yourself without outside support then this is an option to consider. One final thing to mention is that you can opt to have more assistance from one of their realtors. However doing this will add more fees so you won't save as much money as you will if you take care of the open houses and showings yourself. To find a Help-U-Sell agency near you go to their website www.helpusell.com.

Creative Ways to Sell Your House Fast

For Sale By Owner

There is a lot of truth to the saying that if you want something done right then you need to do it yourself. Many times I have done things where I tried to get a partner to help only to find out they weren't as dedicated as I was to reaching our goal. In my life when I attempt to do things on my own then I usually have a group of people (most of whom are family) try to discourage me. Though our family and friends think they are looking out for what's best for us, only you know what is best for yourself. Don't let other's negativity affect your goals, ambitions and aspirations in anything you do in life. Whenever someone has told me that I can't do something, I then set out to prove them wrong. If you have decided in your mind that you absolutely want to try selling your house yourself then give it a try. The worst that can happen is you could fail and waste some time and money, but don't be afraid of failing. Some of the best success stories in history were people who failed multiple times but never gave up. A couple such examples are Abraham Lincoln and Thomas Edison. Lincoln ran for public office and was defeated several times before winning and as you know he later ran for President and won. Edison tried many hundreds of times at inventing the light bulb and failed until he finally got it right. They persevered which is something you may have to do when selling your house in a difficult market. Learn from your mistakes and the financial benefit of success can be a nice reward if you do find a buyer yourself.

According to the National Association of Realtors 13% of home sales in 2008 were done for sale by owner which is more than 1 in every 10. Some people would have you believe you are doing something that very few have done before but that isn't the case. Believe it or not you aren't the only one attempting this out there. In a tough market selling your house yourself might be a better way to go. Realtors can be helpful but they are kind of impartial and they aren't quick to point out the positives especially when the realtor is representing the buyer. You, however, have lived in the house and by showing it yourself will show the potential buyer the pride you have taken in your house. You can point out all the positive things and agree to fix anything they see negative about the house if you wish. When a potential buyer sees a seller who was happy with living in the house it makes it a lot easier for them to see themselves living there and being happy. Make sure you answer questions honestly though. Also make sure to give potential buyers a disclosure form if you had lived in the house. Have a stack filled out and ready to hand out to people when you show your house. If you never lived in the house because it was for investment then you could either do a disclosure alternative form which is shorter or fill out a regular disclosure form which will make the buyers feel more comfortable.

The other great thing with selling your house yourself is you get to avoid having to pay a commission to a realtor. This enables you to be more flexible in the price or in being able to help pay closing costs for the buyer. You may be able to yield a higher profit for yourself. Now I didn't say a higher asking price but rather profit. A good example would be if you are selling your house for $500,000 and the typical real estate commission in your area is 6% then you would save $30,000 (minus whatever you spent on marketing your house for sale) or if your selling price is $100,000 then you would save $6,000. Either way a good chunk of change that stays in your pocket.

When people are meeting you personally it becomes easier for you to be firm on your price. I have noticed that when a buyer is negotiating through a realtor they don't care how much they try and talk the buyer down. Why? This is because they haven't met the seller and so they don't have any connection to them or what they might think. Once you have met the seller then everything changes. You may feel more personally connected thus making it likelier you will give the seller close to what he is asking. This can be especially true if the house is nice and you have decided this is absolutely the house for you and the price is fair. I once sold a house where most people who expressed interest didn't ask if the price was negotiable. Since I was selling it myself I was able to offer a good price that people thought was fair. The people I ended up selling the house to didn't mention price but rather decided to purchase the house for the price I was offering it at. If you are selling and you are trying to get top dollar, then steer away from giving any clues to your potential buyer that you need a quick sale. Don't let them know you are in the middle of a messy divorce or you are behind on your mortgage or you are moving out of state. On the other hand if you really really need a quick sale then go ahead and spill the beans, but if you can I really recommend holding back for at least a few weeks to see if you can get top dollar. When you sound desperate and if you advertise sounding desperate then you will attract investors and others looking for a good deal and no one is going to want to pay full price for your house.

Seal the deal. Once you find a buyer then make sure to get everything in writing right away. Don't procrastinate on this and give them the opportunity to go look at more houses and forget about yours. I recommend to have a purchase agreement ready in case you sell the house to the first person who looks at it. Be sure to get a legally sound purchase agreement form from the lawyer or realtor you are going to have facilitate the closing. If someone really likes your house and wants to buy it then make sure to have them sign a purchase agreement right away and get an earnest money check. If they waver then let them know you have had other calls and will be showing the house to other interested parties while they decide what they want to do.

Tip: When signing a purchase agreement try to limit the number of buyer contingencies to as few as possible. Its normal for a deal to be contingent on financing but make sure to put a time limit within 45–60 days at the most. If a buyer wants the deal to be contingent on an inspection then make sure a time limit is set that they have one week to do so. Don't let them procrastinate and hold you up especially if someone else is interested in the house.

Another factor to consider when selling your house is market timing especially because it's your money being used for advertising. The best time to sell a house at least here in the north is early spring starting in March and April to early summer. Start selling at this time of the year and you are going to increase your chance of success. However selling in the fall or winter isn't going to give you a high probability of selling as the market drops off during this time of the year.

As an investor I go out looking for good deals in the middle of winter. However, most sane people don't want to be house hunting when its 20 below zero and having to walk through 2 feet of snow. In some of the southern states this might not apply as much but if you live in a state where there is snow you will find very few people out house hunting from November through February. The one exception is when you are offering seller financing with a low down payment. Whenever I have offered this in January through March my phone rang off the hook. Why? The reason is because people are getting tax refunds and have money coming that they can put down on a house but they might not have the best credit. Many people take their houses off the market during the winter because they don't want to move so if you decide to try selling it at least you will have less competition.

Be aware of the drawbacks of selling yourself. Even though I am a big fan of selling by owner and I want to encourage you to do the same, there are a few things to be aware of. The biggest drawback is the final sales price. With an agent you are much likelier to yield a higher sales price in the end than selling yourself. However, if you are in a hot market then you will waste a lot of money paying that realtor's commission when you likely could have sold the house yourself just as fast. This is where you will need to weigh whether avoiding having to pay a realtor's commission is going to yield you a higher profit or not. Also, according to the National Association of Realtors, the following are some other common problems that for sale by owners have. The first is getting the house sold within the anticipated timeframe. The next is having issues with getting the house prepared and fixed up so it's in the best possible condition for showing buyers. As to be expected, the next problem is dealing with all the paperwork, but obtaining good forms from a real-estate professional should help you with that. Finally, we are all very busy, so being able to devote enough time to all the aspects involved in selling yourself can be an issue. It is a lot of work, but don't let any of these issues discourage you. Rather, understand what I am telling you and take action accordingly so you will have success.

Your Marketing Campaign

To sell your house yourself you must have a good marketing campaign. This is the number one most important thing you will do when selling. Whether you are selling a house in excellent shape or one in need of repair you won't sell it unless you get people in the door. To get people in the door you must do everything you can to make sure as many people as possible know that your house is for sale. Some people selling their house for sale by owner simply stick a sign in the front yard and think that is good enough. While it may generate some phone calls especially if you live on a busy street it's highly unlikely that making this your only form of advertising will generate a sale. Think outside the box. First you need to write a killer classified ad that will get your phone ringing off the hook. In your ad put a phone number for the phone that you answer most of the time like a cell phone. Do you have a website for your house? If so then be sure to include that in the ad also. When you don't pick up the phone there are some people who may not leave a voicemail and won't inquire about your house again. If you are willing to do a contract for deed and willing to sell to someone with less than perfect credit then you will have an even easier time selling your house. Whenever I have offered seller financing in an ad I have found that my phone rings off the hook and most questions have to do with this. Things to include in the ad besides seller financing are asking price, positives about the house, renovations and upgrades, neighborhood, # of bedrooms & bathrooms, and any incentives that you are willing to throw in such as help with closing costs or carpet allowance, etc. Trial and error can be key to having a good ad. If your first ad doesn't get your phone ringing off the hook or more hits on your website then try something else. Simply rewording the ad or placing an attention grabber can make all the difference. See the examples below of some good classified ads of houses for sale. The first one is for offering seller financing.

Contract for Deed
Seller financing on home with spectacular view of lake on this eastside neighborhood remodeled 4 bdrm/1 bath ranch featuring newer siding, roof, deck & windows. Asking $159,900 with $10,000 down. Call 555-555-5555.

Tip: Always include the area code in case you get out of town buyers calling as most newspapers also run their ads online. Here is an example without offering seller financing.

Unbelievable Lake View
Spacious eastside ranch with view of Lake Erie and remodeled throughout including newer siding, roof, windows and a deck. Offering this 4 bdrm/1 bath with many upgrades for $159,900. Call 555-555-5555.

Here is an example if your house needs work before someone can live in it or just a lot of repairs.

Handyman Special

Must sell quick 2 story eastside home with 4 bedrooms/1 bath and lots of potential. Large back yard and newer garage but house needs a proud new owner to put some TLC in. You won't find a better deal than this at $99,000. Call 555-555-5555.

For anyone that lives in a large market where there are many house for sale ads in the paper I would recommend a very catchy title that is going to make you stand out from the competition. Here is a couple examples but again the key here is to be creative and think outside the box when writing your ad. Advertising is all about grabbing attention by sticking out from the rest of the pack.

Lobster Tonight!

Right on the ocean and perfect for swimming and fishing. Beautiful 5 bedroom/3 bath 2 story house with brand new 3 car garage. No expense was spared inside which features granite countertops, stainless steel appliances, spectacular balcony and much more. Sacrifice at $709,000. Call 555-555-5555.

Hurricane Took Down

The neighbor's house but this solid 3 bedroom/1 bath has withstood it all. Remodeled bungalow features new windows, siding and roof. Newly remodeled dream kitchen and bathroom with Jacuzzi tub. This house in bayside district has it all for only $499,900. Willing to pay 3% of buyers closing costs. Call 555-555-5555.

A Baseball Went Through My Window

Totally redone 3 bdrm/2 bath ranch right across the street from Washington Park. Brand new appliances, newer deck, siding and garage. Spectacular kitchen with granite countertops. Asking $299,000. Bonus big screen tv. Call Frank at 555-555-5555.

There is no limit to the things you can do in your marketing campaign. Next you will want to do some onsite advertising. The most common is the for sale sign bought at the local hardware store. If you want to be like everyone else then go ahead and do this. However if you want your house to really stick out from the rest which is highly important when selling something then I would consider other options. Creating your own sign is certainly a possibility but make sure it looks professional or you can have one custom made by a sign company, just make sure you don't forget to put your website address somewhere on the sign in addition to your phone#. Instead of doing a sign I suggest going a different approach, I am a fan of putting up a huge banner on the front of the house.

Banner I used to sell a house contract for deed.

A great website for ordering these custom made banners is halfpricebanners.com. If you aren't on such a busy street then see if you can put up either a banner on a busy street with an arrow pointing towards your house or a sign with an arrow. Just make sure to get permission for this whether it be from the property owner or your city as you will want to leave them up until the house sells. My banner was bright yellow and even though the house wasn't on a busy street it did generate some calls, as you can see who could miss the thing driving by? If yours isn't going to be bright yellow then at least make sure it's very noticeable and includes catchy things that will get people calling such as offering a contract for deed. Along with your banner or sign if you choose to go that route is to put up a brochure box in the front yard which can usually be bought at your local hardware store. Make up a nice brochure of your house explaining all the important features. This will enable people to learn more about your house and to get a feel for the inside as long as you put some good pictures on it without you having to show it. They can then call you if they are interested in an actual showing and if not then all you wasted was a little money by creating the brochure.

Other advertising ideas to consider are radio adver-tising and the MLS. Radio reaches many people but can get expensive and depending how big your city is this may or may not be effective. One thing I highly recommend is that you put the house in the MLS which is the multiple listing service. This is where realtors place all their listings so this way if a realtor does want to show your house then this will give you one more way to possibly sell it without having to pay as large of a commission. One website that will put you in the MLS for a flat fee is MLSyourway.com. Their fees usually run from about $199 for 3 months, $299 for 6 months or $399 for one year. The advantage to this is you pay their fee and then you can offer a 2-4% commission to realtors if they bring you a buyer versus the normal 5-7% you would be charged if you listed it with a realtor directly. This could save you thousands in commissions plus you still have the freedom to sell to a buyer that you find whereas when you have it listed with a realtor they get the commission whether they find the buyer or you do. A local realtor in your area might also be willing to put your house in the MLS for a flat fee but may charge you a little more. One agent in my area charges $500 for doing this. When putting your house on the flat fee MLS I would recommend sending a postcard to all the realtors in your area letting them know about your house and the commission you are offering. Yes they will see it when it comes across on the hot sheet but this gives another way to get exposure for your house. The hot sheet is the list of houses realtors get everyday that are either brand new listings, expired listings, or a price drop on a current listing. Also don't forget to put a lockbox on the house in case a realtor wants to show your house and you are either not going to be home or the house is vacant. A lockbox is also helpful in case your contractor or the appraiser needs to get in and you are too busy to meet them.

Advertising online is very popular. Some people have listed their house for sale on ebay.com, I have never tried this but it's another idea. Craigslist.org is another website I have used for selling a house and has yielded me a good amount of phone calls. Many people are now using this site for selling everything from household items to cars, boats, appliances, etc. This website has become so popular that the classified section in the local newspaper is continuing to shrink as more people would rather advertise for free online especially since you can include pictures. I have posted my apartments for rent on this site and the house I live in now I found on Craigslist as for sale by owner. After looking at house after house on the MLS with our realtor and not finding what we were looking for my wife and I stumbled across this house which a contractor who had just redone the entire house was selling himself. In addition to the real estate for sale section on Craigslist there is a swap section which might help if you are willing to do this. There are some tax advantages to doing house swaps as well so check with your accountant for more specifics. A lot of people especially younger people are now looking at houses online and if you put your house in the MLS with MLSyourway.com they will automatically include you on realtor.com. Don't forget about social networking sites such as facebook.com which is a cheap way to advertise that reaches many people. Since most buyers are now on the web I would recommend creating your own website showcasing your house. The possibilities with this are endless. You can put up tons of pictures, include audio or video if you want and of course an in depth description of your house.

Here is a story of my friend Lloyd who sold his house doing a combination of facebook.com and craigslist.org. Lloyd had bought a house in a small town in Nebraska. After college, an opportunity emerged for them to go live in Texas and so they moved. However Lloyd had to get his house sold even though he lived in another state. As most people do he decided to initially list with a realtor. A month went by and this realtor hadn't gotten a single person into the house and she should have if she was doing any advertising as the house was very nice. In the contract was a commission of 6.5% for the realtor so you would think that would be motivating. The realtor was making the problem worse by not doing their job as Lloyd had a house he bought in Texas and he really needed to get the house in Nebraska sold quickly to avoid the struggle of trying to make 2 mortgage payments indefinitely. After that month went by he called up the realtor and convinced her to cancel the contract. In the agents defense this was a slow time of year as it was in the winter when the market is usually slow and it was 2008 when the housing market wasn't doing too well either. Right after this Lloyd got to work trying to sell his house by himself and from out of state. He sent a friend over to the house to take over 100 pictures and then he created his own website to showcase his house. On the website he included all these pictures and yes it was over 100, this isn't an exaggeration. He also put a Google map of the house, a very detailed description of each room, and a blueprint of the floor plan which he got from the county.   Lloyd added a video of the house with 3 minutes of audio where his wife described each room and he had an appraisal done and put the entire thing on his website. Every person who called about the house didn't have any questions, they just wanted to see the house. Since he wasn't able to show it himself he arranged for his friend to show the house and to have an open house as well. He put an ad in the local newspaper and a large sign in the front yard. He decided to advertise on the web by putting an ad on facebook.com for around $100 in which he included the whole state of Nebraska and reached about 30,000 people. When you advertise on facebook.com they let you select the demographics that you want to advertise to so it is very helpful to know the kinds of people who might be interested in your house. He was able to include a nice picture of the house on there and started getting calls from people as far as an hour and a half away. One key thing to note is that on all his advertising he included his website address. Lloyd also put an ad on Craigslist however there wasn't one for his little town so he had to put the ad for the town nearest his house which was about a 45 minute drive away. In the end it was the facebook.com ad that got him a buyer, but you never know which method of advertising will find you a buyer so it's best to use as many media outlets as possible. Lloyd's story is a real success story because not only did he sell his house himself while living in another state but he did it in 30 days time which is the same amount of time the realtor had. He also had 2 interested buyers and ended up getting $7,000 more than the appraised value. One thing to note is the appraisal was conservative though because had his house been 3 blocks away it may have appraised for up to $60,000 more. His specific location was a disadvantage due to the blighted industrial park across the street.

One final thing to mention is when putting pictures online whether on your own website or an ad they need to be really nice quality professional looking pictures. I can't take good pictures so I have my wife take them. She knows how to take good shots from just the right angle and using the right lighting to make the house look its absolute best. Don't be afraid to ask a more talented friend or relative to take the pictures for you. To make it even easier I recommend to use a digital camera so you don't have to go through processing film and then scanning pictures only to find out they don't look right on the computer. Most people have a digital camera so borrow one if needed. According to the National Association of Realtors 87% of people searching for a house looked online and of that 77% drove by the house and 63% actually walked through the house that they saw online. Look at these statistics for 2008 from the National Association of Realtors and decide for yourself where you think it makes sense to spend the majority of your time, money and effort on advertising:

1. Buyers are 1,000% likelier to buy a home they found on the internet than from a newspaper.
2. The percent of buyers using the internet to find a home went from 2% in 1995 to 87% as of 2008.
3. A survey conducted of homebuyers asking if the internet is becoming more important than print advertising to market a home had over 94% answer yes.

This also means that a shoddy picture has the potential to drastically cut down the number of people who want to come see your house. Include only 1 or 2 pictures then you have just wasted money also. When you advertise online you need to put as many pictures as possible to give your buyer a feel for the house.

Take a look at some of Lloyd's pictures.

Pick Your Neighbor

Another great marketing technique that you can try is what's called the "pick your neighbor" campaign. Simply obtain a list of addresses in your neighborhood and send a letter, post card or flier to them advertising your house for sale. On the post card or flier you say something along the lines of "how would you like to pick your neighbor and get paid for it?" You then offer an incentive for them to help you find a buyer for you and if they do then after closing you pay them $500–$1000 or whatever you decided on for the referral of a buyer. The other advantage to them is they are picking out their neighbor, someone they know and would like to live near. Maybe mom & dad are getting older and it would be better to have them closer to take care of. Someone at work may be looking for a house and so they tell them about yours. Word of mouth is great and it's a win–win for both parties. Its up to you to chose how many block radius from your house that you would like to advertise to. You can go to the post office and get a mailing list of names and addresses in your targeted postal code. To save money instead of mailing you can simply go door to door (or pay someone to do this for you) and stick the fliers in the doors. When going door to door be careful as the disadvantages are if someone has a no solicitor sign or a mean dog then you might not get to advertise to everyone without getting in trouble or possibly bit. If you have a classified board at work or in your local grocery store then you may also want to advertise there. Also as I said word of mouth is the best advertising so tell everyone you know and as many people as you come in contact with that you have a house for sale and you are paying a hefty referral bonus to anyone who brings you a buyer. Have fliers or business cards ready that you can hand people you meet.   Use email and send a flier to family, friends and co-workers that way. The only big problem about selling a house yourself is all the tire kickers out there. Try to weed out the less serious people by phone and if the house is vacant than tell everyone to drive by first and then call you if they want to see the inside. This will save you a lot of time and energy. When offering seller financing also make sure they have the money for the down payment before you waste your time showing the house unless you are ok with doing something creative to get that down payment. When it comes time that someone has an offer also make sure to get some earnest money preferably 1-3%. Earnest money is simply a small down payment from the buyer saying they are serious about buying your house. In my area of the country houses typically go for $100-$150 thousand dollars and I have gotten by with putting down as little as $500 in earnest money. I don't recommend taking such a small amount though, at the very least try to collect $1000-$2000. That way if they aren't really serious you will know as they won't hand the money over but if they are then they will be happy to write you out a check. Depending on your situation and the buyers you can be creative here. Earnest money doesn't have to be money. It can be anything tangible that you will get to keep whether the sale goes through or not. One idea for instance would be a car. However I do recommend to be leery of people who don't have even this much money as that could be a sign they don't know how to manage it or they aren't serious about buying your house. With tire kickers you could waste valuable time thinking you have the house sold but what is to keep someone from backing out of a deal if they haven't handed you a dime?

Pick Your Neighbor Letter

Dear Neighbor,

My name is _____ and I own the house at _____ in the neighborhood here. I am writing you this letter to see if you know of someone who might be interested in purchasing my house. This would be a great opportunity for you to pick your neighbor. If you send me a buyer who purchases my home outright then I will pay you $500 after closing, or if you send me someone who purchases my house on a contract for deed then I will pay you $100. This house is an excellent deal at $_____ and an excellent way to build equity as the appraised value is $_____. The following improvements have been made recently _____, _____ and _____. I can also provide down payment and closing cost assistance if necessary. Under the contract for deed option I would require $_____ down and the payments would be $_____ per month at ___% interest based on a ___ year amortization. After __ years I will require a balloon payment for the remaining balance owing. Taxes each year are $_____ and homeowners insurance is approximately $_____ per year. There will be additional bonuses thrown in for the buyer of this house. They include a free U-haul rental from within a 100 mile radius of the house and also their choice of a flat screen tv, gas barbecue grill, lawnmower, snow blower or a couch. I can be reached anytime at ___ - ___-____ or by email at _____.

Sincerely,
John Doe

Tip: When sending out the letter it's important that you handwrite both the name of the person who you are sending it to and their address and also your return address. You will want this to be legible so if your handwriting is bad then get someone you know to help you with this. If you don't hand-write the names and return address then less people are going to open the letter. Sales is a numbers game so the less people that know about your house the less chance you will have at selling it. Therefore its important that as many people as possible open up and read your letter. The letter itself can be typed though which is probably best as you wouldn't want to sit and handwrite letter after letter. The reason behind handwriting names on the envelope is simply that if people think it's a personal letter instead of a mass mailing then they are more likely to open and read it.

Marketing in different types of media is crucial to being successful at selling your house. If you are in my parents or grandparents generation then there is a good chance that you read the newspaper. My generation is likely to only look online for a house or anything else for that matter. Nosy neighbors might only find out about your house by driving by and seeing your huge banner or for sale sign. People who listen to the radio all day at work or in their car may only learn about your house this way. Whatever you decide to do make sure to include different types of media, write down your marketing plan and then follow through with it.

Answering The Phone

I answer the phone for a living but for some people answering the phone makes them feel uncomfortable. Try your best to display confidence in what you are telling the prospective buyer and confidence in your house. Right away you need to try and establish trust. When someone works with a realtor they are very likely to trust that person right away because they are a professional who has a license. Selling yourself can initially cause some buyers to be suspicious about you or your house. Don't give quick answers and be careful not to rush people off the phone. Spend some time talking with them and establishing a relationship as the more they like you the more they will trust you and want to come see your house and potentially buy it. This is how sales works. Finding things in common so you can relate to others helps build trust. I trust my insurance agent partially because I like him and part of that stems from him taking a personal interest in me. He asks how my family is doing and I give him a hard time about sneaking away from the office to play golf. Since I like him and trust him I have never had a reason to look elsewhere for my homeowners insurance even as prices have increased. The same goes for the 2 houses that I have bought directly from the owner. My wife and I both liked and felt we could trust the sellers in each case. One seller was a retired firefighter, so because of this we felt comfortable trusting him and the other was a contractor who redid the house we bought from him. When we showed interest he offered to make a list of a few things that he promised to finish for us and then we could come and inspect the house to make sure he lived up to his word. He did and we bought the house. Other phone calls you get might be from people who have already driven by the house but for those who haven't the phone call could be a make it or break it moment. Get them as interested as possible but be honest at the same time. If they are looking for a house with a large yard and yours is rather small then be honest so you don't waste your time or theirs showing it. Be prepared for the most common questions that you will be asked. There are accountant type people and investors who will want you to be really specific like knowing the exact size of your lot and the dimensions of your house and the square footage of the house. The average person though will want to get the feel of the house. Common questions will be what updates have you done? Is there a garage and if so how many car garage? How many stories is the house? What is the number of bedrooms and bathrooms? Is the basement finished off? Do the appliances come with the house? How big is the yard? How big are the bedrooms? Try to paint the best picture possible in their mind about your house both inside and out. People over the phone really want to get a clear idea of the layout of your home so explain where the bedrooms are located and be sure to mention the deck just off the kitchen. Other questions that will arise will have to do with seller financing, how much you will take for the house, questions about the neighborhood and why you are selling. Make sure to highlight positives about the neighborhood especially if they are from out of town. Things like parks, walking trails, or even a dead end street can be very appealing to families with kids. There is also a good chance you will get a call or two from a realtor who wants your listing. Keep these names and numbers as these are sometimes the more ambitious realtors, which is good when you are in sales. Your phone conversation will likely involve a question about the price. I have had people ask me my bottom line, what is the least that I would take for the house in a cash deal? Just remember that if someone gets bank financing then that is technically a cash deal because you are getting all cash at closing it just happens to be coming from their bank. Don't give your house away. If you just started advertising then try to stay firm on the price and explain why you are selling your house at that price.

Determining Your Asking Price

Lastly, price your house right. This can be like a science, because if you are priced too high compared to the competition then you will have very few if any interested parties and you will be wasting your hard earned money advertising. If you are priced too low then people may wonder what is wrong with your house and decide not to pick up the phone and inquire about it or worse you will lose money that you could have made. Since you have decided to embark on this journey yourself instead of hiring a profes-sional then you may have to do a little research or pay to figure out a fair price for your house. Also be mindful if your local market has dropped since you purchased your house. Try not to be in denial about what you think you can get out of your house versus the reality of what others are getting on today's market. One option is to get an appraisal done but this will cost money. If you go this route you could ask the appraiser to do what is called the short form which is usually about half the price of a full appraisal. This is a more con-densed appraisal with a lot less information however if you are simply worried about figuring out an accurate price this may be a good way to go. The great thing about getting an appraisal is you can photocopy the report and give it to prospective buyers who come to see your house. This will also give you a clear idea on how much your house will sell for. If you aren't 100% decided on selling and the appraisal comes back at less than you thought it would then this might be a good time to evaluate if now is the best time to sell your house. Check with your county assessor to find out the assessed value of your house. Generally the value they have on the house is conservative and may not take into account recent improvements that you have made. Sometimes the assessed value is tens of thousands less than what the house is actually worth. Unless your market has declined then you usually would want to price the house for more than the assessed value.

Another way you can figure out a good price for your house is to take a drive through your neighborhood and see what comparable properties are selling for on the market. Go to realtor.com and view other listings in your local area. When doing this try to compare apples to apples and find only those houses that are very similar to yours in number of bedrooms and bathrooms, upgrades, square footage, age of house, lot size and features such as garage, swimming pool, etc. Also try to compare houses that are in your neighbor-hood and, if possible, within several blocks of your house. The reason is that neighborhoods can vary even several blocks away. A few blocks away might consist of homes that are significantly bigger or more expensive than yours or much older or newer. Maybe a few blocks away there is an industrial building and therefore your house is more valuable because your location is more desirable. Another website that is becoming popular and may help you in figuring out a good price for your house is zillow.com. This is an excellent website that helps you estimate the current value of your home for free. This website has data on more than 90 million houses in the U.S. Whether you use the web or drive around just be sure to compare houses as similar as possible in features and location to yours.

The Art Of Negotiation

Now I said that there are buyers who won't talk you down however be prepared to negotiate as it's a very normal part of selling a house. Most buyers will give you an offer within 10% of your asking price. However, there are also buyers out there who may be classified as bottom feeders wanting to get your house for as little as they can. Try not to be insulted if someone makes a low ball offer as it does happen sometimes. Instead, enter into negotiation with them and give them a counter offer that you feel is fair. If the buyer truly wants your house then they will negotiate and you may go back and forth several times to reach a deal so you may not want to go your absolute lowest on the first counter offer. Most houses I have bought or sold have gone back and forth a couple times but eventually we arrived at a deal. Be flexible, as being too rigid in negotiating may kill your deal. Would you want to lose a chance to sell because you won't come down an additional $1000 or you won't throw in the fridge? Your monthly carrying costs could add up to more than that and who knows when the next buyer will come along. Here in the north just heating a house for a couple of months could cost more than this and don't forget about the wasted money you are spending on mortgage interest, property taxes and insurance. Negotiating is part of buying a house so don't set your price too low and be willing to work with your buyer.

Before putting your house up for sale you need to have a figure in your mind that you absolutely won't go below when selling your house. This is a price that you would rather keep the house and stay living there or rent it out before you would sell it for less. Try to figure out the best you can the expenses that I talked about that you will incur at closing and any other expenses you need to recover such as remodeling costs. Decide how much cash you need to get when this deal closes. Depending on your situation it could be a matter of simply getting out of the house the amount you still owe the bank. Adding up your expenses will help you figure out the least you are willing to accept for the house. Don't be disappointed if you can't reach a deal in the end with someone who made an insultingly low offer. If they did this to you then they are going to look at more houses and do the same thing to other sellers. They are the type of person who is trying to get something for nothing and you need to make sure it's not at your expense. Don't be sucked into sob stories as you need to look out for your best interest and that of your family. Especially when you sell your house for sale by owner people will try to play on the emotional factor to talk you down lower than you want to go. Other buyers might only bank qualify for a certain amount and they are trying to get the best house they can afford. Be reasonable when negotiating as there may be things the buyer wants fixed or upgraded so be willing to take something off the price or to take care of some of these things yourself. No house is perfect, but the deal should be a fair one in the end for both you and the buyer.

Being A Salesman When You're Not One

I am a horrible at sales, but that doesn't matter. I clam up at the thought of selling something to someone, let alone selling something as major as a house. I am extremely honest and you need to be also with your potential buyer. This may go against what you believe but it's the right thing to do and will insure a transaction in which you don't get sued later on for something you failed to disclose. You don't need to be the most personable and outgoing person in the world to sell your house yourself. You just simply need to point out all the positives about the house and if reasonable agree to fix anything that needs fixing or negotiate on the price instead. Show your pride in ownership by pointing out all the things you have improved in the house. Be available or have someone available that can show the house at almost anytime. Be flexible, if someone calls you and wants to see the house 10 minutes from now then if possible show them the house. I have done this, its not convenient especially in winter when its 10 degrees below zero but it's necessary. I have dealt with vacant houses so one thing to mention is showings when you are still living in the house. I have heard many stories where people show up at all hours asking owners to let them in to see the house. These people can be very demanding and persuasive making you think you will lose the sale if you don't show them the house now. Be discerning with these kinds of people. If they seem shady then schedule a showing for another day and if they are serious they will come back. If your house looks spectacular from the open house you just held a few hours prior then maybe you will want to show them the house right away. This is up to you but a lot of times if people don't have enough respect for you to come back when its more con-venient then you might not want to deal with them anyway. Are you very busy like most people? You could put in your advertising shown by appointment only. Believe it or not but some people will set up a time and date to come see your house and then not show up. I always ask for them to call me just before they head over to the house so I know I am not wasting my time waiting for them when they may not show up at all. When you show your house give the potential buyer a tour. As I have said this not only allows you to highlight the positives but it will allow you to keep an eye on them in case they are dishonest. Don't leave your valuables in plain site, lest an unscrupulous person walks off with something during one of your showings. I have never had this happen but I have heard stories where it has. For your protection its best to have a sign in sheet that you require everyone to sign when they first walk in.

    In the past I have also leveraged my time by doing an open house. That way you tell people you are going to be at the house from whatever time to whatever time and give them the date (make sure you do this on Saturday or Sunday as that is when most people are available) and they will show up if they really are interested in the house. Sunday afternoon seems to be the very best time but I have done Saturday afternoons before and sold a house this way. Make sure to have a sign in sheet for buyers to sign that you can use for a follow up call later. You don't want to miss a possible sale especially in this market by being rigid with when you are willing to show the house. This means that you need to keep the house picked up and in the condition that you want people to see it at all times while you are trying to sell. I know this can be quite a challenge especially if you have kids (believe me, I know as I have two little ones), but being ready at a moments notice is important. Whether you do individual showings or have an open house make sure to set your house at a comfortable temperature beforehand. Living in northern Minnesota I usually keep the heat down a little low and freeze. In vacant houses to conserve heat I usually keep the temperature around 50 degrees. However doing this for a showing can leave a negative impact on your buyer. You want them to feel comfortable so they go home and remember how nice the house was and not how they were shivering during the showing. Another small thing is to turn all the lights on and to let as much natural light as possible into the house. I have looked at houses where shades and curtains were shut which gave a dark feeling. People like to see houses bright and sunny and have that natural sunlight shining in.

When talking with your buyers there may be times that you might not know the answer regarding a certain aspect of your house such as how many square feet it is but offer to find out and get back to them. Try to prepare a sheet that has pictures of your house along with all the important facts that a realtor would offer if they were selling the house, such as the year the house was built, the amount of property taxes, square footage of each room and a list of improvements that you have made. Just like any other salesman you need to follow up with your leads. This seems like it should be common sense but to some people it's not. When people leave you a voicemail then you need to return the call as promptly as possible. The same with e-mail, you need to check it everyday and reply promptly to inquiries about your house. When people come through your house and seem interested try to get their names and phone number and give them a follow up call a few days to a week later to see how interested they are. Sometimes the only thing holding them back from buying your house is a problem they are having that you can solve. A very common scenario is that they might not have enough money for closing costs but you can offer to help pay closing costs. I once had buyers who looked at one of my houses twice and seemed pretty inter- ested but then I didn't hear from them for over a week so I assumed they weren't interested after all. I then sold the house to another couple on a contract for deed. Several days later I got a call from them saying they went to the bank and got qualified and were still interested. I had to turn them down as I already had a deal with someone else. Not making that follow up call put me in a place that I regret because instead of doing a contract for deed I could have cashed out of the house right away which would have been more ideal for me. Again, I repeat, pick up the phone and make that follow up call so you don't end up regretting it.

Feedback

When realtors show houses they will usually get feedback and send it to the listing agent as to why their buyers did or didn't like your house and why. You should try to obtain some of the same information when selling your house yourself. After you show the house then wait a few days and make a follow up call to not just interested parties but also to those people who didn't seem like they were interested. Ask them what they loved about the house or why they absolutely won't be considering buying your house. Be careful here not to seem like you are pressuring them into buying your house so be sure to explain that you are just doing follow up. I would recommend asking what they liked and didn't like about the house. Ask about their level of interest and be sure to explain your flexibility in making changes to the house and helping with whatever they may need so they can buy your house. Getting feedback will give you valuable insight into whether your price might be too high or whether you need to re-carpet your entire house and dump that orange shag carpet you have had in your living room since the 70's. There will be things that buyers won't like that you can't change like the size of your lot or the size of the bedrooms but constructive feedback can be very helpful to see if there are some little things you haven't done that could be changed to get your house sold quicker. Be proud of the work you did to your house and don't let the nitpickers discourage you. Just remember that the more appeal you can add the better as the more appealing features and positives about the house the likelier that someone will walk in and snatch up your house. Keep in mind that most people don't have vision, they simply want to move in and not have to do anything.

Incentives

The sky is the limit with incentives that you could offer to entice a buyer into buying your house. Be creative, but be aware of the limits of the laws so make sure to consult a real estate professional like a realtor, mortgage broker or lawyer before throwing in any really big incentives. I have heard of people offering expensive cars or nice vacations but some of this can be borderline illegal in some states. Incentives that I would recommend are a home warranty (make sure you put a dollar and time limit). With warranties you have a couple options: one is you can take the risk and pay for any repairs that come up out of your own pocket. The other option is to buy a warranty from a home warranty company. They usually don't cost very much but go a long way to give peace of mind to a buyer. When choosing a home warranty company I strongly recommend that you ask a realtor for a recommendation. Just like any other industry there are good and bad home warranty companies out there. Other incentives that you could offer are furniture like a couch, bedroom set or living room set. Electronics can be very appealing such as a flat screen tv that you buy and have sitting in the house which adds to the visual effect. For some reason buyers and especially first time homebuyers go nuts over a nice sized flat screen tv. Try to avoid paying full price by going to a big box retailer like Wal-Mart and asking if they have a floor model available for purchase as this would cost less than regular price. Another popular incentive is hot tubs. Most buyers love when they see a hot tub. This doesn't mean you need to go out and buy a brand new top of the line one. The general rule of thumb is the incentive needs to be attached to the house and as long as this is the case it should be legal. Just be aware that an addendum to the purchase agreement might need to be filled out to list any incentives you are including with the house.

The other type of incentives are monetary. There is a lot of restrictions especially with lenders on these. However, an incentive that is okay and allows you to help the buyer monetarily is by offering to help pay part of their closing costs. This is probably the most widely used and effective tool and has become the norm with first time homebuyer transactions. Generally the seller is allowed to help with 3% of the selling price of the house towards closing costs. However this can vary depending on the lender and type of loan that is being done. Other monetary incentives that you could consider offering are a carpet or paint allowance, furnishings allowance, garage allowance, roof allowance, deck allowance, furnace allowance, etc. Due to the credit crisis, a lot of banks have put limits to what they will allow when it comes to these type of allowances, as they fear of having the selling price being over-inflated to covers these allowances. Be sure not to go overboard and to double check with the buyer's lender that what you are offering is acceptable.

Making A Smooth Transaction For Your Buyer

The best thing you can do for your potential buyer is having all your ducks in a row to ensure a smooth transaction. Moving can be very hectic and scary if someone is a first time homebuyer. Think back to when you bought your first house and how stressed out you were. Yes, you were probably very excited, but also nervous about all the things involved in having a smooth closing. One thing you can offer that almost no one else does to your buyer is to pay for a U-haul rental for them and order pizza for them and their helpers on their moving day. If you decide to do something like this make sure to include this in your advertising.   See Dan's advertisements on the next page for a house he sold in Moose Lake, MN:

You can also pick out the title company or lawyer that you will close the transaction at. Not all title companies and attorneys are considered equal. If you haven't done business before with the lawyer or title company you are hiring then make sure the lawyer is very experienced in real-estate transactions and that the title company is reputable. Believe it or not but there are some fly-by-night title companies and we have had the authorities shut down a few in our area for collecting title insurance money but not depositing it with the title insurance company. Generally, a business that has been in business for many years can be trusted. Help your buyer obtain financing. There are people in the banking industry who are greedy and will tell their clients anything whether it's in their best interest or not so they can close the loan and earn their commission. This is part of the reason why we are in such a mess in this country with foreclosures, it's because people were misled by dishonest mortgage brokers. If you know of a good banker or mortgage broker that you trust then make sure to refer your buyers to them. This will give you peace of mind about the long financing process and also helps you by pushing your buyers another step closer to closing on your house. I have an excellent mortgage broker whom I love referring people to and I know that he will get the job done and do everything according to the law. Also, if you have or know of a good insurance agent then refer your buyers to them. A lot of first time homebuyers are strapped for cash, I know I was. Find out if your insurance agent will take monthly payments for the home-owners insurance policy. If so, this could really help out a prospective buyer who is cash-strapped. All this not only makes a smoother transaction, but you may also get a small reward from the banker or insurance agent for referring them business. Plus going the extra mile may be what is needed to get your house sold in this difficult market. When I bought my first house my realtor referred me to an excellent mortgage broker who I have used ever since. That mortgage broker in turn referred me to a great insurance agent who I still use today.

Traditional Bank Financing

The most common way to sell a house involves the buyer finding their own bank financing. You might be lucky enough to get a true cash deal where the buyer has enough cash for the house which makes for a really quick closing but more often than not the deal will involve a bank. Once you have a deal on paper with your buyer then the purchase agreement needs to be sent to their bank or mortgage broker. These little details would normally be handled by a realtor, however, when you are selling yourself you will need to take care of a few more things to keep the transaction rolling along. I should mention that if you don't feel comfortable doing this then you could hire a realtor who will charge you a fee to assist you in some of these closing details. It's best that before you sign a purchase agreement that the buyer has been pre-qualified. If not then send them to your bank or mortgage broker to get pre-qualified right away.   That way you aren't pulling your house off the market and wasting time selling to someone who might not be able to buy your house.

I strongly recommend getting financing through a mortgage broker over a bank as they are more likely to get the loan closed with as good or better interest rate for the buyer than a bank will. A mortgage broker works with many banks and sometimes even hundreds of them and works to find the best deal for his client. The disadvantage to the buyer is they could end up paying a little more in closing costs. This might be more than offset by a better interest rate which saves more in the long run versus the rate your buyer would have gotten at their local bank. Many local banks tend to be more conservative and might require a larger down payment or a better debt to income ratio than a lender that your mortgage broker finds would require. I also recommend that you establish good communication with the buyer's lender and make sure their banker or broker is up front with you regarding any problems that might prevent the deal from closing. Privacy laws in your state may limit how much they can tell you but try to find out what you can.

I wish I could say that there aren't problems and that everything goes smoothly in real-estate transactions, but that isn't the case. Sometimes everything goes smoothly and sometimes the banks nitpick. Ever since the credit crisis the banks have gotten more conservative on who they will lend to and they are checking everything with a fine tooth comb whereas before they were lending to anyone who had a pulse. Try not to get frustrated if something doesn't go according to plan or if the closing gets bumped back a couple weeks. The most recent house we bought ended up taking just over 2 months to close when under normal circumstances it should have been about 5-6 weeks at the very most. What happened is the sellers we were buying the house from were investors and they bought the house with cash as a foreclosure. Well, they fixed up the property so quick and the banks are so bogged down with foreclosures that the title hadn't been transferred into their name yet in the county records. This was a problem for our lender as there are scams out there so they wouldn't close our loan until this title issue was taken care of even though we were getting title insurance. Make sure you have a set closing date in your purchase agreement, usually within 45 days. Depending on the situation maybe you will agree to extend beyond that but I wouldn't initially commit to more time then this in your purchase agreement. Please keep open communication with your buyer as well and make sure to follow up with them several times that everything is going according to plan. When selling your house if you have multiple interested parties then make sure to take back up offers. You never know when or if a deal will fall apart and if you have a back up offer than that is all the better for you. Multiple offer situations were very common in many parts of the country when the real-estate market was good however now they have become rare in most markets but they do still happen sometimes. The buyer's banker or broker will usually take care of some of the details like picking out a title company or attorney to close with. After turning the purchase agreement in to the lender also find out where the closing will take place unless you are picking it out and make sure to hand the earnest money deposit over to the attorney or title company. This will take it out of your hands and also put the buyer more at ease.

Wrapping up your end of the bargain is important with bank financing. This is important no matter what but especially when the bank is controlling the time line for closing and trying to get the deal to close as quick as possible which is good for you. Make sure you have taken care of all the details you promised regarding fixing things or making improvements in the house. If you promised to build a deck then get this done as soon as possible. Regarding utilities, make sure you have paid all your bills current as some states have laws in which the delinquent utility bills can be attached to the property thus creating a problem for you. Assessments are something else you should be aware of. Most transactions done through a realtor require you as the seller to pay the assessments to your property and a for sale by owner transaction should be no different. Assessments are liens attached to the property through your county and billed on your property tax statement. These can be for a street or sidewalk that was redone in front of your house or an unpaid garbage bill. Be honest and up front with your buyer about assessments. You can certainly negotiate these as maybe they would be willing to pay part of it if the assessment was for a street repair as they will be reaping part of the benefit. Not disclosing assessments and not planning on taking care of them is going to come back and bite you at closing, as the title company or attorney will discover this when they are doing a title search on the property.

Fees At Closing

Every time I have sold a house I seemed to be in shock at the fees I ended up paying at closing as the seller. The settlement statement never seems to end up in my favor as much as I had in my mind by running the figures in my head. The good faith estimate by the bank is for the buyer, and the seller is usually left to wonder what extra costs they will have at closing. Here are some things to expect you will end up pay at closing. If you hired a realtor then you will have the realtor's commission come right off the top which would be $5000-$7000 for a 5-7% commission off every $100,000 you sold the house for. An example would be if your final selling price was $300,000 and the commission was 6% then $18,000 comes right off the top to your realtor. Next is interest owed to your bank if you have a mortgage. Interest is paid in arrears not in advance. Here is an example, let's say you made your last mortgage payment on June 1st and the closing is on June 15th then you will owe interest to your bank from June 1-16th because your last payment covered interest on your loan from May 1-31. The reason for the extra day is your title company will overnight the check to your bank to pay off the loan and you owe interest until they receive it. Depending on how much you owe, at what interest rate, and how long you have had the loan will all factor in and can add up to hundreds or thousands of dollars. If you want to know what to expect then look at your last mortgage statement as it will show you how much of your last payment went towards principal and how much towards interest. Let's say your last statement showed that $650 of your payment went towards interest. Using the above example you would owe around $347 worth of interest at closing which is $650 divided by 30 days in a month for $21.66 per day x 16 days= $346.66. Don't forget you will also owe the remaining principal balance of your loan on top of this. As I talked about before, the property taxes are generally prorated and this along with assessments will generally be subtracted at closing. Don't forget about the portion of the buyers closing costs that you agreed to pay. An example would be the final agreed upon selling price for your house is $200,000 and you agreed to pay 2% of the buyers closing costs, calculate 2% of $200,000 and you would have another $4000 gone off the top. Other costs you may be on the hook for are title insurance and a recording tax for recording the sale with your county. Depending on your state or city there could be other fees that the seller is responsible for. All these fees can add hundreds more to the total taken off that final check that you will get at closing.

I recently sold a house and as usual I was surprised at all the fees I had to pay as the seller. Everything was listed on a settlement statement and the representative of the title company explained each line. The following are some of the fees I had to pay. The buyer's lender charged me a $100 inspection fee. There was also a title search fee, title examination fee, document fee, wire fee, recording fee and state tax. When it was all said and done these misc. fees added over $900 to my closing costs. All the charges were legitimate and I learned my lesson to inquire ahead of time next time before the closing.

Tip: Call a realtor or title company to get an idea of how much closing costs are in general for the area you live in and based upon your selling price. This way if you have just a small margin to work with when selling your house you won't be shocked at closing.

Laws & Permits

Make sure you are aware of real-estate laws, especially those governing the sale of a house in your area. There are state laws that differ from state to state which you can find out about through your attorney or though your states department of commerce website. Some cities have local laws or require certain inspections to be done prior to the close of a house. Here in Duluth, MN, we have a law that the water & gas division of the city has to come in and determine whether the house needs a sump pump or not prior to the sale of a house. This is due to a sanitary sewer overflow issue that our city is having. After you have the inspection they give you a certificate stating you had this done. If your house requires a sump pump then there are grants available to cover the cost. The title companies in our area are aware of this law however if you as the seller aren't then you could potentially hold up your closing by failing to have this done in a timely manner. Any work you are doing on your house that usually requires a permit I would recommend that you follow the law and obtain one for those projects. Most buyers hire a home inspector and many times they will check for permits for the work that you claim was done on the house especially if you or the contractor did less than a perfect job. Don't leave them wondering why you didn't pull permits, you might kill your sale. There are also disclosure laws in most states that you need to be aware of. Even though I have included a disclosure form in this course for you to use you still might want to run it by an attorney to make sure it's not missing anything. One example is some states require sellers to disclose if anyone has died in the house. For some people knowing this is very important. I think it's a little crazy, however, you don't want the neighbors telling your buyer something that you didn't disclose and have it come back and bite you later on.

Uncle Sam

What would a book about real-estate be without a chapter about taxes? Most reading this book may be in a position where they must sell or have decided for sure they are going to sell. For those of you who haven't or for those who are curious as to how bad Uncle Sam is going to sock it to you at tax time, please read on. Real-estate is treated as an investment just like if you invest in the stock market or anything else so it's therefore subject to capital gains tax. There is a very nice tax loophole that the federal government gives on owner occupied properties. When you live in a house that is your primary residence for 2 of the last 5 years and then sell it then you don't have to pay capital gains as long as your profit is less then $250,000 if single or $500,000 if married. Your profit or gain can be figured out by subtracting the price you bought your house for + improvements from the selling price. You also don't need to have lived there for 2 consecutive years to be capital gains tax free. You could have lived there the first year you bought the property, then moved out for 3 years and then back in for the last year. An example for figuring out your profit would be if you sell your house for $600,000 and you had originally purchased it for $200,000 and you made $40,000 in improvements. Take the $600,000 − $240,000 ($200,000 + $40,000) = $360,000 capital gain. If you meet the residency requirement and you are married then, you are tax-free on this capital gain. However if you are single then you would owe capital gains tax on $110,000 as only the first $250,000 would be tax free. There is an exception to the 2 year residency requirement if you need to sell sooner due to unforeseen circumstances, such as having to move because of a job transfer or medical issues. When this is the case the IRS allows you to take a partial deduction. An example would be if you were forced by your employer to move to another city and you just bought your house 1 year ago. If you are married you would then be able to claim half the $500,000 deduction which would equate to $250,000 or if you are single it would be $125,000. If you don't have an unforeseen circumstance then the general rule of thumb holds true that if you sell a house you owned for less than a year then it will be treated as a short-term capital gain. This means you may be subject to paying taxes based on what-ever income bracket you are in. If you hold the property for more than a year then it would be subject to the long-term capital gains tax. Currently the long-term capital gain tax for those in the 10% and 15% tax brackets is 0%, however this is set to expire at the end of 2010 unless Congress extends it. For the income brackets higher than this the current long term rate is 15%. Many people are building wealth by buying a house, living in it for 2 years and then reselling it and then doing the same thing over and over again every 2 years. There is no limit as you are allowed to take this exclusion every two years so if you don't mind moving and you are ambitious enough to do this then go for it. This is a great way to make enough money to eventually pay cash for a house and buy your dream home. Being mortgage-free has a few advantages. The greatest is peace of mind, but the other is you aren't paying all the interest each month to the bank as a 30 year mortgage in the end will end up costing you double the original purchase price. As always, please speak with a professional tax advisor relating to any tax questions as the above information is a guide and tax laws continue to change each year.

Seller Financing

The Contract For Deed

A sure way to sell your house many times faster especially in a slow market is by offering seller financing. The most common method for doing this is by selling on a contract for deed. A contract for deed is simply a document that transfers ownership from one person to another. The

two parties agree and then sign an agreement that determines the purchase price, interest rate and payment terms of the deal. If you know you are going to offer this then don't waste your time or money by hiring a realtor. If you do then you are going to have to reach in your own pocket for the commission or use up all the money you got down from the buyer with no guarantee that the buyer will follow through with the terms of the contract for deed. Contract for deeds used to be kind of rare, but due to the credit crisis they are becoming increasingly more common. Now many buyers who would have bank qualified for a house before aren't, and many sellers aren't able to sell conventionally so more contract for deeds are being done. This can be an excellent way to go and can yield you a higher selling price. However there are drawbacks including if the buyer just disappears one day or stops paying you and stays living there, then you have a huge hassle to deal with in getting them out and essentially you have to foreclose on them. Generally, foreclosing on a contract for deed transaction means that you cancel the contract due to the buyer failing to abide by the terms of the contract. This process is usually around 60 days in most states versus a traditional foreclosure with a bank which can be 6-12 months. A huge drawback is that your buyer could also damage the house extensively either purposely or simply by neglect. Some extreme signs of neglect and carelessness that happens is they smoke in the house and thus yellow the walls or they have a dog or cat that urinated inside and ruined all the carpet. Another common problem that arises with seller financing trans- actions is you get to the end of the term that you set and are ready to receive your balloon payment from them but they tell you they need more time. You in turn end up extending the contract for another year and then another year until who knows when. Depending on the situation you could opt to sell the house to someone else as they breeched the contract by not coming up with the money to cash you out. I always recommend to work with people and try to come up with a solution but mention this so you know its within your rights to do this. Some options to consider in a situation like this are asking for more money down and or increasing the monthly payment to accelerate the contract. However, when a contract for deed works it works very well and can be a very attractive source of monthly income especially if you owe very little or nothing on the house you are selling. To best protect yourself against these kinds of problems you need to do a few very important things:

The first is get as large of a down payment as possible. I live in an area where homes typically sell for $100k–$150k and recommend asking for $5000–$8000 down in this price range which is about 5% of the selling price. You may live in a totally different market so you need to figure out your comfort level when deciding the down payment amount that you will require. Very likely you already know what you are going to use this money for so that will help you determine the amount. If you have a really nice house then asking for 10% isn't too excessive but remember the lower the down payment the more people that will be able to purchase your house. Next you need to do some research and find out more about who you are dealing with. Start by running a credit check. This doesn't necessarily mean you are going to turn them down due to their less than perfect credit. It does however give you insight as to how big a risk they might be based on their credit history. If they have judgments against them then maybe you will want to turn them down. Remember, you are acting as the bank here. Otherwise if you do want to go through with the transaction then maybe you will want to require a larger down payment and/ or charge them a higher interest rate since they are a higher risk. I have included a form with this course that you can use for screening potential buyers.

Before determining the interest rate that you will charge your buyer there are a few things you should know. Uncle Sam sets a minimum interest rate and a maximum that can be charged. The only time you might want to be at the minimum is if you are selling vacant land, selling your house to a family member, if you are doing a really short contract like 6 months, or if you are selling to an investor as a last resort. To find out the minimum rate required by law if you decide to go this route you should either contact the IRS, a

CPA or an attorney. Deciding on the interest rate is very important because if you set it too low then you are giving your buyer no reason to ever balloon the payment and get you the lump sum of cash you are waiting for. I would recommend charging 2-3% higher than what the bank is currently charging for a mortgage and, like I said, if you think your buyer is high risk then charge even more.

Most states have laws that set a maximum interest rate that can be charged on these type of transactions so check with an attorney or title company about this. Make sure to set the interest rate high enough so that you are making a spread between what the buyer is paying you and what you are paying the bank. Let's say that your payment is $650 a month and your interest rate is 6.75% and you are selling them the house for the $100,000 that you owe. I would recommend setting the interest rate at 8.75% and I always recommend amortizing the payment over 25 or 30 years which would give them a monthly payment of $780 (over 30 years) in this case. You would then cash flow the difference of $130 a month. Make sure that the number of years mirrors what your mortgage is so if you have a 30 year loan then you wouldn't want to do a 25 year amortization with your buyer. If you do then they will be paying down on the principal that they owe you faster than you are paying down your mortgage. This could result in you owing your bank more when the balloon comes due than what the seller owes you. To figure out an amortization schedule you can go to yahoo.com or bankrate.com as well as many other sites. I once did a contract for deed where I owed around $57,000 on the house and I sold it for $84,900. After the down payment of a little less than 10% of the purchase price the buyers owed $76,700 which I then amortized over 25 years at 7.95%. My loan was amortized over 25 years also but at 6.5% (I was going to charge them 8.5% but lowered it slightly since they put more down than I was asking for). Their payment to me was about $589 per month and my payment to the bank was about $397 so I had a positive cash flow each month of $192. In the contract they need to come up with a balloon payment in 5 years for the remaining balance. However we did write a clause that would allow then to extend the contract for an additional 5 years. For the extension they would have to put an additional $1000 down towards the principal. There are some investors out there who simply buy houses to flip them on contract for deeds as they supply a good stream of monthly income but without the hassles of renting to someone. Over time you build up more of a profit on the property if you structured the deal right. Your buyer is also building up equity if the house increases in value. Charging your buyer a higher interest rate than what your mortgage is can put more money in your pocket.

See my illustration below:

For simplicity the first amortization schedule is a contract for deed in which you sold the house to your buyer for $100,000 and charged them 9.5% interest amortized over 30 years. I show only the first 5 years assuming you will balloon it at that point.

Year	Beginning Balance	Interest	Annual Payment	Ending Balance
1	$100000	$9474	$10090	$99383
2	99383	9412	10090	98706
3	98706	9345	10090	97960
4	97960	9271	10090	97141
5	97141	9190	10090	96241

This second table is your loan with your bank for $80000 at 6.5% interest amortized over 30 years.

1	$80000	$5174	$6068	$79106
2	79106	5114	6068	78152
3	78152	5050	6068	77134
4	77134	4982	6068	76048
5	76048	4909	6068	74889

As you can see in the beginning there was a $20,000 gap between what your buyer owed you and you owed your bank. After 5 years that gap has grown to $21,352 allowing you to pocket some extra money when your buyer cashes you out. This example also would have given you a positive monthly cash flow of $335. I recommend using the mortgage calculator on yahoo.com to run your numbers and make sure you are structuring your deal right.

There are some creative ways for you to get a down payment from your buyer. Just like any other seller I prefer to get as big a down payment as possible. However, given the current state of the real-estate market you may need to be creative at this just as you are using a creative technique to sell your house. I recently sold a house and took $200 down (I don't recommend taking this small of an amount down) and wrote in the contract that I would get an additional $8000 as a balloon payment within 120 days. Where was this $8000 coming from you might ask? Well, my buyer happened to be a first time homebuyer and qualified for the $8000 tax credit. Since I was skeptical about a seller financed transaction qualifying for the credit I decided to call the IRS myself to check. It turned out that yes contract for deeds do qualify for this tax credit. The first time homebuyer's tax credit can be filed for right away instead of waiting until you do next years taxes. After originating the contract for deed they filed for the tax credit and within 120 days I got my money. Now this particular tax credit is set to expire in June of 2010 unless the government decides to extend it again. Many people who have kids get large tax refunds so an ordinary tax refund could be used the same way. Other ideas can be based upon your creativity. What are your needs as a seller? Have you always been wanting to go on a dream trip to the Caribbean? If so, see if your buyer has a credit card that they can pay for your vacation on as the down payment. Is there new furniture you need? Are you moving across the country? Do you need an extra car and the buyer happens to have a great extra car they were thinking about getting rid of anyway and could give you as the down payment? Maybe you don't need the extra cash right now and you have very trustworthy buyers with good jobs. If so, could you spread the down payment over 24 months by adding an additional $200 per month to the payment which would be $200 x 24 months= $4800. Ask the buyers if they have family or friends or an asset that they own that they can borrow against at the local bank. I bought my first house by borrowing against my car which I owned free and clear. The buyers might be a little reluctant but they might have options where they can borrow against their 401k or life insurance policy. Again, be flexible and creative as the sky is the limit, but don't be willing to take on a risk you can't handle.

Potential pitfalls to being creative with the down payment and seller financing are you have little protection if things go wrong. If you have potential buyers and they say they are expecting a settlement then beware as this is a huge red flag as they are basically waiting on something that may never happen, like waiting to win the lottery. Job history, if it's not stable then I wouldn't recommend taking the risk. Obviously there are different situations like a couple might be retired but generally look for stable income. Rental history, call their prior landlords to find out if they've had any evictions or problems making on time rent payments. You can also do a check of court records at your local county courthouse to find evictions and criminal history to see who you are dealing with. Make sure to do your due diligence when assessing taking a risk on someone as things can and do go wrong sometimes with these transactions. Here is a story where Dan Quade sold a house out in the country to a family and he got an $8000 down payment, however one day they stopped paying him. He decided to go to the house and investigate after he was unable to reach them but they were long gone. To make matters worse it was winter and they left the house unheated so some of the pipes froze which created a disaster for him. Thankfully he had insurance and was able to get the house repaired and was then able to resell to someone else on a contract for deed but not without going through a great deal of hassle and stress.

The other great thing with doing a contract for deed is you don't have to hold the note until the end of the contract. A note is what you created when you decided to do seller financing and created the contract for deed. You can turn around and sell the note to an investor and get out of it right away or hold it for a period of time and then sell it. Generally, an investor may offer you 50–90% of the face value of the note but depending on what you want out of the house this could be a good deal for you. Let's say you sell your house on a contract for deed for $100,000 then an investor would offer you anywhere from $50,000–$90,000 to buy the note. Depending on the deal you negotiate it can be a good deal for both you and the investor if you are wanting to get all your cash out of the property and be done with it. If you end up in a situation where you are short on cash then you could sell part of your monthly positive cash flow for a lump sum payment. This allows you to get more money faster but at the same time not giving up any of the principal balance.

Recording the contract for deed with your county is something I highly recommend. This protects you and can help you if you decided to sell the note. Some note buyers look for these opportunities and may send you an advertisement offering to buy your note. The way they found you is by the contract for deed being recorded with the county. I have gotten these postcards before but I have also seen investors who advertise in the local paper that they will pay cash for your contract for deed note. Otherwise, if you decide to hang onto the note and you found a good buyer, then sit back, relax and savor the fact that you are making money each month off the spread of what they are paying you versus what you owe the bank and the best part is that you don't have to do any land lording. If you do hold a mortgage then make sure you are aware of the due on sale clause in your mortgage. This states that your bank can call your debt as payable immediately because of you selling the house, which you are technically doing by originating a contract for deed. One other tip I have is to set up an account at your local bank that your buyer can deposit their monthly payment to you in each month. This will be easier for you as you won't need to wait for a check in the mail and then deposit it and also this gives proof that they paid you on time each month which they can give the bank when they go apply for a mortgage.

Be sure to set up your contract for deed with a lawyer or a knowledgeable title company. This will protect both you and the buyer. Things to be discussed and included in the contract include improvements. You need to set a dollar limit regarding changes they can make to the house before they need to notify you. The general rule of thumb is a small amount like $500 but you can do what you want. I would include a clause that they can't alter the structure at all or knock down walls without your written consent first.

Occupancy should also be discussed. If you don't want to allow them to use it for a rental then make sure this is included in your contract. Its very important to find out your buyers intent for your property. Property taxes and insurance should be figured out and discussed in the contract. There are two ways to do this. One is you can escrow them where they are divided equally between 12 months and paid to you along with the payment and you then turn around and pay the taxes and insurance to their proper entities. This is the best way to protect yourself. Just make sure you remember to recalculate the payment each year as property taxes will likely increase and possibly the insurance. If you escrow with your mortgage company then you will most likely want to go this route. However, if you own the house free and clear or don't escrow now then you could have the buyer pay the property taxes and home-owners insurance directly. Either have them send you a copy of the receipt after they pay as proof or follow up with your county assessor to make sure the taxes are being paid. For the insurance make sure that your mortgage company is still listed as loss payee and that your name is included on the policy in the event of a loss. It's generally best to try and keep the insurance with your current agent however if the buyers choose to get their own agent then make sure this is set up correctly and that you are getting duplicate notices. The fair thing to do is prorate the property taxes and if the property is non-homesteaded then you may end up being responsible for that portion of the taxes as well. Assignment could be an important issue, even though you as the seller can assign the note you probably don't want to allow the buyer to assign their interest to someone else.

If you are selling the property "as is" and your property is less than perfect then make sure that an "as is" clause is added to the contract. This is included so you don't get phone calls all the time that this or that went wrong and the buyers having an expectation that you need to fix it. One way to further protect yourself in regards to this would be to have a home inspection done prior to you trying to sell your house. This will cost you a few hundred dollars but there are a couple benefits. One benefit is that you know exactly what is wrong with the house and can fix these things or negotiate as needed. The other benefit is that it gives the potential buyers more peace of mind and saves them money by not having to hire their own inspector. You can photocopy the home inspection report to hand out to prospective buyers who come to look at your house. Most buyers will hire their own home inspector. If they do then don't let the inspector kill your deal as I have had happen to me. Home inspectors are hired to find things wrong however they are not supposed to put a price tag on work that needs to be done. I had an offer from a couple and the home inspector told them the house needed $20,000 in repairs so they backed out of the deal. When professional contractors came after to estimate repairs it turned out that to fix everything it was only going to cost less than $5000. Make sure if the buyer hires their own home inspector that you speak with him after the inspection to get a clear understanding of what he thinks is wrong with the house. Also make sure you have included in your purchase agreement the amount of repairs that you are on the hook for prior to the inspection. If the home inspection comes back with a higher amount of needed repairs then you can negotiate with your buyer. A good real-estate lawyer is going to include and mention all this so make sure you hire someone who knows what they are doing.

Rent To Own

Lease options, also known as rent to own, can be a very quick way to unload your house. Many would be buyers out there are interested in going this route if they may have no credit, bad credit or have been foreclosed on but don't want to throw out their money by just renting. With a lease option you can design it many different ways but typically it works like this: you find a buyer who agrees to rent your house for a specified amount of time, generally 2 or 3 years. You agree on a purchase price to sell the house to them at and draw up a contract with a lawyer. Part of the monthly rent goes towards their down payment if they obtain their own financing within the specified period of time. When home values are going up this can be a very attractive deal for the buyer as they are building up equity. Generally you want to charge them a premium price each month versus what would have been charged had you rented the place instead of doing a lease option. If the buyer fails to obtain their own financing or if they choose not to exercise their right to buy it then you get to keep the money they paid you each month as rent and if your contract also states, possibly their down payment as well. Down payments on lease options are usually very small. Take note that a lease option is just that, it gives the buyer an option of whether to buy the property or not, they are under no obligation to do so. They can simply walk away at the end of the contract and have no repercussions.

An example would be that you are selling a single family house for $80,000 and you find someone who agrees to do a lease option with you at $1000 per month. Had you rented the house in your market you likely would have gotten $800 per month. You agree that if they purchase the house within 2 years then 50% of what they paid you each month will go towards the purchase price. Though 50% is very typical you can design the contract how you want. You can include a clause to extend it out another year after that if you would like. If home prices in your area are going up about 3% per year then at the end of 2 years the house will be worth almost $85,000. Since the buyer was locked into the $80,000 price they gain just about $5000 in equity from the house appreciating in value. They also gain equity from half the monthly payment that is going toward the principal which in this case would be $500 x 24 months=$12,000. Now they can go to the bank and get a loan for the remaining $68,000 they owe you ($80,000–$12,000) and they have 20% equity since the house is worth $85,000 (20% x $85,000=$17,000) so the bank is now much likelier to lend to them. The sky is the limit, it's up to you to decide the terms you want.

Rent to own can be very attractive for you especially if you have a less than perfect house that isn't likely to sell on the market for what you owe. Do you have a house that you are tired of renting out and getting bad tenants consistently? I recommend to put a little work into the house so it doesn't look quite like a rental. Try to create some curb appeal but don't spend a lot of money. Then try selling your house on a lease option which may be a better route to go in your state versus doing a contract for deed. Check with your attorney on this. Getting even $1000 down is better than being a landlord especially if your house is in a bad neighborhood. Using a lease option can give you a very nice positive cash flow each month and allows people with bad credit to have an opportunity to buy a house. Finding good people is key and this can end up a win-win situation. When people are buying a house like this they tend to take more ownership and fix things themselves versus if you rent the house then you end up Land lording and have to deal with all those hassles. I own rental property and Murphy's law is definitely true with tenants as I have seen anything that could go wrong end up going wrong many times. As always I will talk about the drawbacks to doing a lease option because there are pro's and con's to everything. Typically with rent to own you don't get a lot of money down, a lot of times the amount equal to first months rent as kind of a security deposit. That means you have less of a cushion if they decide to completely trash your house and take off. It also means if they fall behind then you could quickly end up in the hole if you still have a mortgage on the property.

The other drawback is you are typically dealing with people who maybe shouldn't be buying a house and might not ever qualify because they can't get their lives together financially. This means if you were really hoping they would find financing and buy your house then you may end up very disappointed when the contract ends and their credit is still in the dump. Make sure you are aware of your state laws as some states may require you to have a certain amount of equity to be able to do a lease option. As with a contract for deed its also best to record the lease option contract with your county. Since this is technically a lease you as the seller are usually responsible for major repairs to the house during this time. Generally you would also be responsible for the property taxes, homeowners insurance, assessments and private mortgage insurance. Just as you would with a contract for deed make sure to discuss who will be living in the property, and if you don't want your buyer leasing the property out to someone else then make sure to include a no sublease clause. I highly recommend that you don't allow the buyer to assign their interest in the contract either as allowing this or subleasing can create a messy situation later.

Lease-Purchase

Yet another option to consider which isn't commonly used is a lease-purchase which is very similar to a lease option. The difference would be that you sign an actual purchase agreement that the buyer is going to go out and get financing within a very short period of time like 6-12 months. Until your closing date you are agreeing to rent the property to the buyer. This is a selling technique that is used to get a buyer into the house to cover your monthly expenses but delay the closing while the buyer wraps up whatever they need to do to get the financing. Some buyers wanting to do this with you might have a house in a different city that they need to sell before they can obtain a mortgage on your property. Under this deal no part of the rent would go towards the down payment so it's in the buyer's best interest to hurry up and get things in order to close.   Should you decide to go this route then I highly recommend getting a large earnest money check up front. This will help ensure that the sale will go through in the end because you are pulling the property off the market and taking some risk here. Going this route can be more attractive than a lease option because of the short time frame. Just be sure that the buyer is doing what they promised in getting their credit in order or their down payment together or whatever they needed to do so you can close.

Pre-qualifying Your Buyer

A few years ago at the height of the housing boom I would have been laughed at for writing a chapter like this but in today's credit market it is very important to cover. If you are unsure of whether to offer selling financing or not here are some things to consider when running credit checks and pre-qualifying your buyers. A buyer may not have the best credit and if it's really bad meaning under 600 then you would most certainly have to either do a rent to own or contract for deed if this buyer is your only option for getting rid of your house. If their credit is 600-650 there is hope that they might bank-qualify in the future to buy your house, but they will have to work at rebuilding up their credit some more. These people are prime candidates for a contract for deed. For someone who has credit over 650 it's highly likely that they will be able to get a mortgage. Generally, I highly recommend encouraging your buyer to work with a mortgage broker versus a local bank. The reason is that they are more likely to get approved for a loan versus having to bounce from bank to bank trying to find someone who will approve the loan. Each bank will pull credit which will knock a few points off their credit score, thus lowering their chances each time. A mortgage broker on the other hand works with many banks, sometimes even hundreds of them. They can usually obtain a very competitive interest rate for their clients. The one drawback is closing costs will probably be higher than dealing with your local hometown bank which tends to eat some of the closing costs. Local banks tend to be more conservative and may require more money down than a mortgage broker would, which could be a problem if your buyer doesn't have that extra money to put down. Suppose the buyers credit needs some fixing before they will qualify for the loan then a good mortgage broker should be able to tell them what needs to be done before they can be approved for a mortgage. If the mortgage broker can't approve them then they usually gives a copy of the buyer's credit report to them so they know exactly what needs to be cleared up to improve their credit. Everything from the past that may have been forgotten about could be showing up like unpaid medical, credit card or utility bills. To fix any of these negative things on the credit report they would call the number listed and pay off the debt if possible. If not then maybe they could try to get a loan at the bank or from a family member to pay off any old debts. Once these old debts are taken care of it still may take a month or two before it reflects on the credit report. Another thing that can look bad is if they have too many inquiries on their credit report or very little established credit which is usually a history of accounts being open less than 3 years. Job hopping looks bad especially to the local bank which may require being in a current job for 6 months before lending. A mortgage broker on the other hand can usually do 1-2 months as long as the past job history is stable. Banks, and even a mortgage broker, will require a 2 year history before they can count commission income. I know it doesn't seem fair but that's the way it is and I have ran into this problem in the past myself.

Creative Ways to Get Rid of Your House to Avoid Foreclosure

Auction Your House

Depending on your level of desperation, equity and condition of the house an auction might be a quick way to sell your house. Real-estate is auctioned all the time. For instance, when counties sell tax-forfeited land and houses they hold a public auction. Banks also hold an auction called a Sheriff's sale when a house goes into foreclosure. With that being said, it's usually the bargain hunters who attend real-estate auctions so be prepared to sell cheap. If you want to try an online auction then Ebay would be the best way to go. I have looked at real-estate on Ebay but I have always been skeptical at buying on there. However, the fees are reasonable and it's another way to try selling your house. You can either do an auction where people bid on the price or you can list it at a fixed price so it may be a cheap way to advertise. Otherwise you can hire an auction house to sell your house. Just make sure the company is reputable and that they have auctioned off real-estate before. Generally, an auction house will take a specified percent of the final sales price. If the fees are too high and if you are really ambitious you can certainly auction off your house yourself. You could either set it up as a silent auction where people submit silent bids on paper or a regular auction where you are yelling out the price. To auction the house yourself I would recommend doing a marketing blitz by putting a classified ad in your local paper and advertising online on Craigslist as well as putting fliers around town. Set up a date ahead of the auction date for people to come and inspect the property and also some time on the day of the auction for people to arrive early and look at the property. This could be a very good way to go if you have a house that is condemned and needs to be torn down as the house has no value, just the land. Just be aware that if you hire an auction house then you will be bound to the bidder for selling the house and you will owe the auction house a fee. However, if you auction the house yourself and accept bids and nothing is acceptable then depending how you run the auction you may not be bound to the high bidder. Just make it clear before the auction that you reserve the right to refuse any and all bids.

Deed In Lieu

Deed in lieu's weren't very common before the mortgage crisis. Very few people know about or have heard about a deed in lieu. This is an agreement between you and your bank that you will hand the title back to them without stalling or putting up a fight, or in other words, a voluntary foreclosure. If you are behind in payments and know you will be unable to catch up even if you were to do a loan re-workout with your lender, then I would recommend trying this option. This can be a better alternative than having to file bankruptcy or go through an actual foreclosure. However, if you would like to stay in your house and think you can catch up or get your lender to work with you then you might want to see if your bank will do a loan re-workout or mod-ification with you instead. This is becoming more and more common especially now during the credit crisis as banks are overloaded with the number of foreclosures they have. Just be aware that doing a loan modification is also likely to damage your credit as lenders typically report this to the credit bureau. Before doing a deed in lieu your bank will probably require you to list the house up for sale with a realtor for at least 90 days. They do this because they want you to prove that you can't sell your house before they will be willing to do a deed in lieu. If you aren't behind on your payments and want to simply give the property back to the bank then good luck, usually the bank is only willing to consider this once you're behind. You need to know that the bank really doesn't want your house back as it's a huge hassle for them to deal with in addition to the money they lose. A deed in lieu is worth trying because if the bank accepts this deal with you then you may be able to salvage your credit somewhat versus going through a foreclosure where you will destroy it. The deed in lieu will show up on your credit report and damage your credit badly but not nearly like a foreclosure would. This could also help you stem off a possible bankruptcy. The other disadvantage is that if you decide somewhere down the road to apply for a home loan in the future then you will likely be asked if you have ever done a deed in lieu which may result in a denial for the loan or a higher interest rate. So if you can sell your property you are better off doing that and trying a deed in lieu as a last resort. Another word of advice, if you are behind on your payments and unsure what you are going to do at this time then stay in regular contact with your bank. Explain your situation and try to work out a solution. The worst thing you can do is hide and not answer the phone when they call. It may be a good idea to consult with an attorney before going this route to see if a deed in lieu is the best option for your situation.

Short Sale

Banks are increasingly accepting short sales. A short sale is when you sell your house for less than what you owe. Typically this happens when you are behind in payments and you find a buyer, however the buyer's best offer is still less than what you owe on the house. Sometimes a seller is in a position where they have enough cash to cover the difference however more often than not the seller doesn't have the difference to pay the bank. Other common situations where people might end up having to sell their house short would be an unexpected job transfer to another city, divorce, a landlord who is fed up with dealing with trouble tenants and simply wants out, or other situations where a quick sale is necessary. The bank doesn't want to end up foreclosing so they may agree to forgive the difference by doing a short sale especially if the seller is a few months behind in payments. The thing to be aware of is that you could be on the hook for the difference leaving you owing the bank money for a house you no longer have. Depending on your situation and ability to repay this money this could push you into bankruptcy. The reason for this is the bank can come back and get a judgment against you for this money and have your wages docked unless you set up an acceptable repayment plan. I would highly recommend contacting your lender prior to considering a short sale and talking with the loss mitigation department. You may be able to work out very favorable terms to repay the difference. The bank could potentially forgive the whole difference and that can and does happen however there are some drawbacks. One huge downside is if your bank decides to forgive the difference, then the forgiven amount could be considered taxable income.

An example would be that Frank & Sally have a home and owe $220,000 on their mortgage, they are behind by 2 months and home prices have declined in their area since they purchased their house 2 years ago.   Luckily they find a buyer who loves their house and gives them an offer. However the house only appraises at $200,000 and both Frank & Sally and their prospective buyer want to proceed with the sale but it will be for the $200,000 the house appraised for. This creates a real problem for Frank & Sally as they both lost their jobs in the recession and obviously they don't have an extra $20,000 just laying around other-wise they wouldn't be selling. Fortunately, their bank allows them to proceed with the short sale and given their circum-stances, decides to forgive the full $20,000 (beware not all situations end up this happy). The loss mitigation depart-ment at your bank will assess your financial situation and determine whether you are able to repay the money or not. Besides missing the 2 payments the short sale itself may have negative consequences on Frank & Sally's credit report. Frank & Sally move on with their lives but the last thing they will need to do is bring this to the attention of their professional tax accountant to see how this will impact their taxes because the forgiven $20,000 might be considered taxable income. The other downside to doing a short sale is the amount of time it can take. Many realtors aren't willing to take on listings that may result in a short sale because it can easily take 6 months or longer before the transaction goes to closing. They don't always take nearly this long but it can, it depends a lot on the lender. Selling yourself in a short sale situation isn't likely to have any quicker results so you need to make sure you have a very patient buyer who really loves your house. There are so many foreclosures right now that banks are simply bogged down with a massive workload so it takes a long time to get through the short sale process.

Tip: When trying to do a short sale (or a loan re-workout) it's important to write a good hardship letter. Explain to the bank not only your situation but also point out why they don't want to take your house back. I recommend acquiring information regarding your local real-estate market to give to your bank if you are dealing with a big national bank. This can simply be newspaper articles that talk about how bad the real-estate market is in your area. You can also ask your realtor for information showing the average number of days a property in your price range has been staying on the market before selling. Any information regarding the number of foreclosures in your area is also helpful. When the bank takes a property back not only will they lose at least what they would by doing a short sale but they also will have to pay a realtors commission, pay for utilities, taxes & insurance and someone to clean the property out.

Here are some examples of an ad you could run if you really want to go this route.

Short Sale! Divorce Situation!

Getting divorced and must sell now. Owe $150,000 but willing to negotiate short sale. Spectacular 3 bedroom/1 bath house in Uptown District with many updates. House built 5 years ago. Call 555-555-5555.

Must Sell Short to Avoid Foreclosure!

My bank will look at any reasonable offer. Owe $210,000 but bank will take less. Remodeled bungalow with 4 bedrooms/2 baths and newer 3 car garage, updated siding and kitchen redone 3 years ago. Located in the Watertown neighborhood. Call 555-555-5555.

My Bank Says Bail Me Out!

Behind on payments and my bank is willing to do short sale. Owe $335,000 and bank will consider reasonable offers. Beautiful house with view near lake. Traditional 2 story with 3 bedrooms/2 baths and huge yard. Many updates throughout. Call 555-555-5555.

Call An Investor

You may have seen signs all over your town as well as the classified ads by real estate investors wanting to buy properties quickly. These are the "I Buy Houses For Cash" ads. Give them a call when you see these ads. They could be the answer to your problems or maybe not, but you won't know unless you place the phone call. Generally, investors are looking for a good deal and in return you get to be rid of your property very quickly so it can be a win-win situation. If you're in a situation where you need to sell quick due to foreclosure, divorce, moving, death of a loved one, etc., and you have a decent amount of equity in your property, then pick up the phone and call. Even if you don't have a large amount of equity you might be able to get your bank to agree to a short sale to the investor or to negotiate attractive terms for the investor. Properties that are in dire need of repair can make really good candidates for investors, especially if you don't have the time or money or motivation to fix up your house to sell on the market. A lot of times if you don't have much equity an investor may still be willing to buy your house based on the terms you offer and you may do a sale on a "subject to". This is a creative buying technique that investors use to acquire properties quickly with little money out of their own pocket. How it works is the buyer takes over your property at the price you agree to with them.

Most commonly it is for what you still owe and the sale is "subject to" an existing loan which stays in your name and is deferred being paid in full until the buyer obtains financing. During this deferral the buyer is responsible for making the payments. Generally this can be a win-win situation as long as you don't care that the loan stays in your name for awhile as investors typically will try to flip the house instead of obtaining their own financing. This can be good for you because "subject to" transactions are usually done really quickly, sometimes in less than a week. If you are struggling with making payments this can give you immediate relief. Also, if you are behind in payments the investor will be required at closing to bring your mortgage current which also helps your credit. Other advantages are you will avoid paying a commission to a realtor and also avoid paying closing costs. Here is an example. Suzie bought a house 5 years ago but has fallen on hard times because she got injured at work and had to take a job earning a lot less than before. She can no longer keep up with her mortgage and is 2 months behind. Between her job and watching her 4 kids she doesn't have the time nor money to sell her house herself and she has no equity so she can't afford a realtor. She desperately wants to save her credit to buy a more affordable house in the future but she owes $250,000 on her mortgage and doesn't know what to do. She puts the following ad in the newspaper:

Take Over My Payments $0 Down
Beautiful 3 bedroom/2 bath home in newly developed
uptown district. Home built 5 years ago with many amenities
and huge backyard. Behind on payments and must sell now.
Call 555–555–5555.

Luckily, a professional young couple are interested and want
to buy the house. They haven't established enough of a
credit history to bank qualify, however, they do have enough
cash to pay lawyer fees and catch up Suzie's mortgage so
they agree to do a subject to sale. In a subject to sale you
have to sign ownership over so that is what Suzie does. This
couple then makes payments and Suzie is out of a bad situation and has saved her credit. Assuming the investor or
home buyer makes the payments on time then this will
improve your credit over time. You also save yourself time
by not having to show the property over and over again to
people that may only be half serious about buying your
house. When dealing with investors make sure that you deal
with a reputable and honest one. There are a lot of greedy
people who will want to take advantage of you because of
your situation. You have worked hard to make those payments so don't be willing to just surrender your equity
because you are desperate. Check with your bank to see if
you have an assumable mortgage. Not many of these were
done after the 1980's, however if you have one then it's even
less risk to you if you can get the mortgage completely out of

your name right away. You can then create a real estate note for the difference of what the investor agrees to give you for the house versus what you owe. A note is simply an IOU. A good example would be if you agree to sell the investor your house for $200,000. You have an assumable mortgage with a balance owing of $150,000, the investor assumes this mortgage and you then create a real estate note (make sure you do this through a lawyer to protect yourself) for the remaining $50,000. You can structure this anyway that you want but make sure that you get some sort of return on your money as you worked hard to build that equity. Maybe ask for 4–7% interest on the $50,000 with him paying you $400 a month amortized over 30 years with a balloon payment in 3–5 years. A balloon payment simply means that after the 3–5 years is up then whatever he still owes you on the $50,000 comes due. At that time he needs to find his own financing and give you a lump sum payment for the balance. I highly recommend amortizing notes over 30 years because then you are collecting mostly interest on your money which is safer and better than if it was sitting in the bank as both savings and CD interest rates are in the toilet right now. Figuring this out is very simple. What I personally do is use the mortgage calculator on yahoo.com.

What To Do If You Still Can't Sell Your House

Every house out there can sell, however it's a matter of what price it will sell at. A house is just like anything else for sale in that it is only worth what someone else is willing to pay for it. No one wants to over pay, especially for a purchase and investment as big as a house. I have placed offers and counteroffers on houses and gone back and forth several times before reaching an agreement. Other houses I have walked away from after my offer wasn't accepted because it wasn't worth it to me to pay what was being asked for the house. On the flip side, I have also paid full price without negotiating when I thought the house was worth every penny and more than the seller was asking for it. Since many sellers in the current real-estate market may not be able to get what they want or need out of their house, there are a couple options as a last resort. Inevitably, the market will pick up and appreciate again as it always has historically, it's just a matter of when. Here are a few final suggestions if you have done everything you could and your house still won't sell. Please note that some of these options could cause a drastic hit to your credit. However, if you already have damaged credit then that might not matter. Don't limit yourself to what I have suggested. Be ambitious and brainstorm to find a solution to getting your house sold. Your house just like any other on the market will sell but not for a penny more than someone is willing to pay for it.

Swap Your House

Swapping your property could be very beneficial especially if you are looking at staying in the same town. This can be a great way to get rid of your house for something that will better fit the needs of your family. A great example would be that you have a one bedroom house and you need a three bedroom for your growing family. You then find someone who is willing to swap who now has an empty nest and wants to downsize. However, this can be very hard to do as you need to find a property you want along with a person who wants to trade you and take your property. Given the state of the current real-estate market though, there are a lot more people who are trying this. A couple websites that you can post your house to swap is domuswap.com or Craigslist. I have also seen people advertise this in the local paper. Generally how a swap works once you find someone to trade with is you would originate a new mortgage on their house in your name at the same time they do one on yours. If you're wanting to defer capital gains taxes then this could be a great route to go through doing a 1031 exchange. This gets a little more complicated as you need to name a possible swap within 45 days of selling your property. For doing a 1031 exchange the property also has to be an investment property, the law doesn't allow you to do this on your principal residence. Just remember you will eventually owe taxes once you sell the new property unless you do a 1031 exchange again. Ask your accountant for more details.

Rent Your House

I know that for me personally renting my house would be a last resort as I know the kinds of problems that renters cause. However, if you owe more on your house then its worth then this might be a good way to ride out the storm until the housing market recovers. Just make sure that you thoroughly screen people. I always recommend doing a criminal background check and a credit check. You also need to call their references and past landlords. However I wouldn't bother calling their current landlord. The reason is if the tenant caused a lot of problems then the landlord will want to get them off his hands so he might be lying when he is saying good things about them. Have prospective tenants fill out a rental application also. Get as much information as possible from prospective tenants including where they work, how long they have worked there, how much income they have per month, who all will be living in the house with them, other monthly expenses they have like a car payment.

Getting all their personal information is also important such as date of birth for the background check and social security number for the credit check. An emergency contact also helps in case there is a real emergency which happened to me when a tenant burned down one of my duplexes. This emergency contact can also be helpful if the tenant skips and still owes you rent. You will be able to get an address of where to send the court summons when you sue them for the rent they skipped out on.

Subdivide

Subdividing is dividing up your house into multiple units to sell or rent separately. Subdividing your house may not be the most practical solution, however if you have a large house you might be able to divide it into condos and sell that way especially in a very good neighborhood or if your house has a spectacular view. Do you have a huge extra lot or two attached to your property? You could sell these lots off separately thus allowing you to ask less for your house and possibly raise much needed cash. Do you have a large house that could be subdivided into rental units and turned into a cash cow of an income property? This could be an option to consider if you live in an area where there are very few rental units and rents are very high. After doing this you could decide whether it makes more sense to keep the property for the income its generating or to sell it which you originally wanted to do. Do you have a rental property that you have been unable to sell? You could turn the rental units into townhouses and sell them individually. Before doing any subdividing make sure to check with your city regarding zoning restrictions and permits for doing this. I also recommend to consult with a real-estate agent as well as a couple contractors to determine whether the investment would be worth doing this. Many people have made big money in real-estate by converting a property into something other than its original use. Subdividing may give you the solution you have been looking for to get rid of your property.

Business Purpose

Homes that are zoned commercial could be transformed into a business purpose. Depending on how large the house is, maybe you could create office or retail space down below and have apartments upstairs. Even if your house is in a residential only zoned area you could lease it to a group home or an assisted living company. Group homes and assisted living companies are popping up all over the country. The group home companies provide 24 hour housing to people with disabilities. The assisted living companies also provide seniors housing so they can live independently but with some help instead of having to go to a nursing home. Often companies starting up have a hard time getting bank lending so this might be a win-win situation. Before converting a house into business space make sure to determine whether your investment in doing so will pay off. Check your newspaper to see how much office and retail space rent for in your area. You may find out that you are better off creating apartments instead of office or retail space. Also check with your city to find out zoning laws and what you are allowed to do when converting a property from one use to another. Changing your house to another use could be the solution you are looking for and might increase the value of your house.

A Crazy Idea That Some People Have Tried

A crazy but creative new way to sell a house that some people are doing is by holding a lottery or contest to win the house. I highly discourage this as there are better ways to sell a house and I am against gambling. I simply mention this because it is happening out there and can serve as an inspiration toward creativity. Should you decide to do something like this then please check your state laws before proceeding as some states outlaw this as it could fall under anti-gambling laws. Here is how it works. You set up a trust or another third party who will handle the financial aspect of the lottery or contest. This entity will be responsible for collecting all money from ticket sales or entries to the contest. You then decide how many tickets you will issue and at what price. An example would be that the house you are selling needs to sell for $200,000 so you decide to issue 2000 tickets for sale at $100 each. You then choose a date for the drawing and advertise like crazy hoping that people will buy all the tickets. Then if all goes well you have the drawing and you have creatively gotten rid of your house. Besides being crazy the biggest drawback is there is a good chance that you won't sell enough tickets or have enough entries to get what you need out of the house. If that happened you would need to have your trust refund everyone their money. This could be a real hassle and could cost you money in fees from the entity over seeing this for you as well as postage. I read a story online of one person who attempt-ed to do this and they put a little different spin on it. Instead of having an actual drawing they had a writing contest with a panel of judges. The fee was $100 to enter the writing contest and the winner of the contest won the house. Not many people will attempt to sell this creatively but let the story inspire you to find a solution that will work best for your house and your situation.

Bonus

To The Property Flipper

As an investor I have learned about some valuable resources I would like to pass on to anyone who is buying this course and is either a property flipper, wants to become one or maybe wants to score a good deal on their next home purchase. Some places to find great deals would be on local or national websites or through the government. Fore-closures have typically been great deals for investors and I found one foreclosure that I ended up buying on the site www.govsales.gov. This is a federal government website that links a lot of resources for the government onto this one page. In order to find houses for sale on this website you would need to click on the tab that says houses and from the map select your state and then your city. Both HUD and VA foreclosure listings can be found here. The best part is that its free and you don't need to register like you do with all those other websites wanting to charge to give foreclosure information. Your county may have a website or if not a list that you can obtain by calling the assessor of tax forfeited properties. Some counties will give you a list of people behind on their property taxes that you could then call or send a letter to see if they are willing to sell. Generally after someone falls 5 years behind on their property taxes the county will confiscate it so I recommend to get a list of people maybe 3 & 4 years behind. You can also try your city and see if they have a condemned property list and a list of former rental properties that were shut down because the owner failed to make repairs. A lot of these properties can be bought cheap and you just might find a diamond in the rough among them that doesn't require substantial work.

Investors looking to find the best deal possible may try advertising to find that good deal. You could place an ad in your local newspaper saying "I Buy Houses for Cash" or "We buy houses and can close quickly". I have other investor friends who have found rock bottom deals doing this. Give it a try and see what happens. You may also offer finder fees to friends, family, co-workers or anyone else that gives you a lead on a super good deal. I have typically heard of investors giving $500–$1000 per property in finders fees. Putting signs around town at busy intersections saying "I buy houses" can generate good leads. I have a friend who puts small signs at intersections that are visible to people sitting there at a red light. If you have decided on target neighborhoods that you want to buy a house in then you could try putting sticky notes on doors saying you are looking to buy a house in the neighborhood. I recommend to have these printed up at a print shop to look professional and also insuring that it's legible as handwriting can be hard for people to decipher sometimes.

Conclusion

Sell your house creatively and put forth a great effort and it will sell. The best success may come from trying a few of these techniques and seeing which gives you the greatest response. Different people respond to different types of media when it comes to advertising. You may reach a young person online but a retired couple might see your ad in the local newspaper. Get the word out to your neighbors and everyone that you know that you are selling your house. Don't be afraid to offer seller financing especially if you are on the verge of losing your house and need to get out quick. Like I said before though, just make sure you are cautious and do checks on the people buying from you if you offer seller financing. Be creative and explore other resources as Dan and I don't know everything and there are many more resources that will give you ideas on how to sell your house. Whatever you do please take action and do something about your situation. The worst thing you can do is think and think and think and think and think and then not do anything about it. Stick to the 90 day rule of trying something else if you didn't succeed in the first 90 days. Think outside the box and don't just copy what other people are doing to get their house sold. We wish you the best of luck on getting your house sold.

www.ingramcontent.com/pod-product-compliance
Lightning Source LLC
Chambersburg PA
CBHW051518170526
45165CB00002B/512